Contents

LAWPACK

bins

A Parent's Guide to the Law
by Jon Robins

© 2009 Lawpack Publishing
Lawpack Publishing Limited
76–89 Alscot Road
London SE1 3AW

www.lawpack.co.uk

ISBN: 978-1-905261-19-2

Valid in England & Wales. The law is stated as at 1 December 2009.

Exclusion of Liability and Disclaimer

About the author

Jon Robins is an award-winning freelance journalist and author. He has been writing for the national press for over ten years. His work has appeared regularly in *The Times*, the *Observer*, the *Guardian*, the *Financial Times, the Daily Express* and *Sunday Express.* Jon writes widely but specialises in writing about the law and consumer issues.

Jon has written several books including *The Justice Gap: whatever happened to legal aid?* (Legal Action Group, 2009) and *People Power: how to run a campaign and make a difference in your community* (*Daily Telegraph* and Lawpack, 2008).

Please note

This book relates to the law of England and Wales only. I have tried to ensure that the information contained here is as accurate and as up-to-date as possible at the time of going to press. But readers should note that the law is in a constant state of flux and subject to constant revision both in our the courts and by Parliament.

Further, please be aware that the book seeks to illuminate the legal issues around different areas of a parent's life. It is not aiming to offer definitive advice (that would not be possible given how quickly the law evolves). Readers are advised to check with the organisations listed in the book and, if needs be, go to professional legally qualified advisers. The book is not a substitute for legal advice.

Introduction

This book is about 'parenting and the law' and considers the legal framework within which we and our children live today. For parents, the bringing up of children should be one of the most important experiences of our lives and, for our children, the quality of our parenting is certainly one of the greatest influences upon their lives for good and for ill.

Raising a family is an experience filled with joy, love and devotion. It is also about hard work and, inevitably, periods of great anxiety as well as concern for the happiness and well-being of our offspring. We live in a complex world where our lives and the lives of our children are prescribed by the law, rules and regulations, which all have a direct impact on us as parents.

A Parent's Guide to the Law is written in a Q&A format and seeks to provide concise explanations for those legal issues that relate to you and your children, offer straightforward and practical advice, and signpost you to reliable sources of help. The book's subject matter follows the journey of parenthood from expecting your first child ('You want a home birth but your local health authority "doesn't do" home births - do you have the right to insist?') to becoming a grandparent ('What about caring for your children's children? What rights do grandparents have?') and all points in between.

Fortunately most of us rarely come into direct contact with the legal system, other than when we move house or get divorced. So readers might well be surprised at the degree to which today's family life has become enmeshed in the 'law'. Depending on your point of view, the predominance of law in our family life may be evidence of necessary and sensible safeguards or (more likely) may represent a convincing case for a 'nanny state' that too often oversteps the mark.

The law as it relates to our children consistently treads that fine line between protecting their best interests and unnecessarily intruding upon our lives and the lives of our children.

A Parent's Guide to the Law features numerous examples of that legislative tightrope. Just to pick one example, at the time of writing, ministers are being forced to rethink a controversial scheme to vet some 11 million adults who are in regular contact with other people's children after a public outcry that such moves could jeopardise 'perfectly safe and normal activities'. The introduction of the so-called 'vetting and barring' scheme followed the inquiry by Sir Michael Bichard into the murders of Holly Wells and Jessica Chapman in the Cambridgeshire town of Soham in 2002. Ministers proposed that failure to register by those who are involved with children through schools or clubs, including volunteers, could result in a fine of up to £5,000. The government insisted that dropping off your friends' kids at school wouldn't be affected but, such is the sensitivity of the issue, the furore was instant. An almost unanimous press chorus from the tabloids to the broadsheets condemned it as an excessively 'paranoid' response to the threat of child abuse which would – in the words of one columnist – 'poison relations between adults and children by treating every grown-up as a suspect'. Society yo-yos dizzyingly between the impulse to use the law to protect with the best of motives and the tendency to resist over-regulation in our lives.

So, life is complex and the bureaucracies that parents have to negotiate are increasingly difficult. The dearth of publicly available information about legal and consumer rights even in the age of the Internet means that parents often feel at a loss as to know where to turn for help. To take one example, in chapter 4 we consider the relatively new phenomenon of school appeals. In 2008 it was reported that more than 100,000 children were denied places at their first-choice secondary school and almost half of families in some areas of London were apparently likely to have been frustrated in their attempts to secure their first choice. Every year, over 50,000 parents go through the appeals system and this has spawned a 'school appeals' industry as anxious parents are increasingly willing to pay lawyers or specialist services to help them, (*Daily Mail,* 3 March, 2009). The aim of this book is to explain to parents how these kind of legal processes work so that parents can make informed decisions as to their rights and those of their children.

For all the press reports about the growth of our compensation culture, ignorance of legal rights – or, just as dangerous, a failure to appreciate the absence of rights – should be of greater concern to our political masters than the corrosive impact that the bringing of unworthy claims allegedly has on society. To take an example of a widespread failure to understand the law, increasingly we choose to live with our partners without getting married and foregoing the legal protections of marriage. It is reckoned that over four million of us live together as man and wife without being married. There are many great reasons to marry or to register a civil partnership (not least, the legal protections they offer); but equally there are many equally compelling reasons not to take that trip down the aisle – we consider them in chapter 9. The problem is that many of us who don't get married wrongly believe that after a couple of years we magically become 'common law' husband and wife, with the same protections as married couples. We don't. The notion of the 'common law wife' is a myth. Our persistent failure to appreciate that lack of legal rights is a source of untold misery for many people when their relationship breaks down.

Divorce is one of the most striking examples of how the law touches upon our lives. Breaking up is hard to do, as the old song goes, but there is plenty of evidence to suggest that the legal process of divorce – its uncertain costs, time-consuming nature, and adversarial nature – only adds to the bitterness and acrimony. Since 1971, the overall divorce rate has doubled (and the number of marriages has halved). According to the Office for National Statistics' figures in 2004 more than four out of every ten couples getting married were likely to end up divorced (45 per cent). People who have been through a divorce often complain about the lack of information available to them and the lack of decent legal advice – and yet so many of us go through the process. The lack of a coherent government policy on the promotion of legal rights at a time when the legal aid system is under such pressure (only 29 per cent of us are now eligible for legal aid) is a shocking oversight.

There are many fantastic organisations which do provide advice to parents and children – many have been involved in the researching of this book, providing material and checking the information. They offer invaluable sources of advice which I urge readers to make full use of. This book is no substitute for the kind of advice they offer.

Finally, I'd like to thank my own family – my wife, Juliet, and two daughters Bea and Eve.

I hope you find the book useful.

Jon Robins
September 2009

Acknowledgments

There are a large number of organisations and individuals I need to thank for their help in the writing of this book.

Chapter 1

I am grateful to the Childrens Legal Centre for helping with information on parental responsibility, and to Katy Swaine, the legal director at the Children's Rights Alliance for England, for her help with the section on children's rights.

Chapter 2

I would like to thank Beverley Beech, chairwoman of the Association for Improvements in the Maternity Services, for her help with the sections on home births and consent for medical treatment; Dilly de-Ville, a midwife of 12 years' experience based in Brighton, helped out with the sections relating to pregnant mothers; and Manuela Da Costa-Fernandes and her colleagues at the Royal College of Midwives helped with the first section of this chapter.

Caitlin J Delaney, an associate solicitor at Irwin Mitchell, provided material for the section on accidents at birth. Many thanks to Mark Tarran, solicitor and editor at PLC Employment, who wrote the sections on employment rights. Susan Seenan, at the Infertility Network UK, provided information on donor insemination and surrogacy as did Natalie Gamble, a partner at leading fertility law firm Gamble and Ghevaert LLP.

Thanks also to the British Association for Adoption & Fostering for providing material for the sections on adoption and fostering.

Chapter 3

I am grateful to the National Childminding Association for its help with this chapter as well as the National Day Nurseries Association for its assistance. Nanny Tax provided information on employing nannies (www.nannytax.co.uk).

Chapters 4 and 5

I am grateful to Margaret McGowan, a journalist who specialises in writing about education, for her help in both chapters 4 and 5. Margaret wrote much of chapter 5. John Chard helped with the section on school admissions in chapter 4. Thanks also to Ann Newstead of Education Otherwise for her input on the home education section.

Chapter 6

Thanks to the National Society for the Prevention of Cruelty to Children (NSPCC) for its help with the sections on babysitting and smacking. The information on protecting young people online comes from the Child Exploitation and Online Protection (CEOP) Centre. Thanks to CEOP for allowing us to use this.

I am grateful to Amanda Stevens, head of personal injury and clinical negligence at Charles Russell LLP, for her input on the law of negligence. Thanks to the Department for Transport for allowing us to use information on the law relating to young drivers. Steve Dennis, former head of Business Development at the BIIAB, assisted with the material on nightclub security. The information contained in the sections on consent to medical treatment, a parent's right to consent and sexual offences were provided by Brook, which provides free and confidential sexual health services and advice for all young people under 25. The NSPCC provided information for the section on sexual abuse.

Chapter 7

Thanks very much to Citizens Advice for its help with the information on young people and money and PJ White, a specialist journalist who runs the excellent site www.youthmoney.com. The British Banks Association assisted with the section on bank accounts and credit cards. I am grateful to Scottish Widows for its help with the section on saving for your children.

I am grateful to the TUC workSMART for allowing use of its material for the section on young people at work. Thanks to Jennie Walsh at the law firm Thompsons and Ian Hart, child employment manager at Surrey County Council, who also helped on this section. Ian provided help and information for the section on employment of young people in entertainment.

The Children's Society and Shelter assisted with the section on young people leaving home. Thanks to Adam Fullwood of Garden Court North for checking. Many thanks also to Liz Fisher-Frank, at the Lawyers for Young People service based at the Children's Society, for writing the section on young people and care.

Chapter 8

Thanks to Andrew Keogh, a criminal defence lawyer and editor of *CrimeLine*, for his help with this chapter, and to Paul Tawn, a criminal defence partner at Fisher Jones & Greenwood, for his assistance with the section on when parents might need legal help.

Chapter 9

Thanks to David Hodson, solicitor, mediator and deputy district judge of the Principal Registry of the Family Division in London, for reading this chapter and for his helpful input. James Pirrie of Family Law in Partnership LLP was also a great help. Thanks also to the family lawyers' group Resolution for their assistance.

I am grateful to Mary Webber and the Advice Now team for their combined help on the section concerning cohabitation and Jo Shortland, of the law firm Oliver Fisher, who provided information for the section on unmarried couples and their homes. Citizens Advice provided the material on wills and intestacy. Stephen Lawson, a litigation partner at Forshaws Davies Ridgway LLP, assisted with the section on the CSA; and the section on domestic violence was written by Ben McCormack and Kate Stone, Garden Court North Chambers.

Thanks to the Grandparent's Association for its help on grandparents and contact issues.

CHAPTER 1

Rights and responsibilities

As any parent knows, bringing up children is more about the 'responsibilities', or duties you have to act in the best interests of children, rather than any kind of 'rights' that you have yourself.

We all have an understanding of what it means to be 'a parent' informed by a mix of our cultural inheritance, family experience, our own intuition, as well as an understanding of what society expects from us. However, the law has some very specific ideas.

For a parent to be able to act as a parent in many situations he must have what is known as 'parental responsibility'. This is a legal concept which is referred to repeatedly throughout the book.

The over arching legal framework for the law as it relates to children is contained in the Children Act 1989, which was described by Lord Mackay, who was Lord Chancellor, at the time as 'the most comprehensive and far reaching reform of child law … in living memory'. In the past, the law treated children very much as the property of their parents rather than individuals in their own right. Arguments over custody, care, control and access were fought over in the courts with the parents' views being the prevailing interest. The Children Act seeks to put the needs of children to the fore of family law. Before the 1989 legislation the law would often refer to 'parental rights and duties', or some such phrase, which is a notion that jars with the experience of parents (surely parenting is about 'responsibilities' rather than 'rights'?). In 1982 the Law Commission noted: 'It can be cogently argued that talk of "parental rights" is not only inaccurate as a matter of juristic analysis but also a misleading use of ordinary language.'

So this chapter begins with a discussion of the concept of 'parental responsibility', which allows us as parents to make important decisions about our children's life. We consider who has parental responsibility (you, your partner or both of you) and how other people (such as step-parents, grandparents, civil partners and other family carers) acquire it. This section then goes on to consider situations when it can be crucial to know who has parental responsibility (e.g. if you want to change your child's surname or take your child abroad). We also look at when parental responsibility ends.

Having looked at what it means in law to be a parent, the second section of this chapter considers what it means to be a child under the law. In particular we look at the legal rights which are largely enshrined in international law which seek to protect children.

Parents

What does it mean to have 'parental responsibility'?

This means that you, as the mother or father, can make important decisions about your child – for example, you can name or change the name of your child, decide their religious faith or, should they have an accident, give consent to emergency medical treatment.

Unlike mothers, fathers don't always have 'parental responsibility'. 'Parental responsibility' is defined under UK law as 'all the rights, duties, powers, responsibilities and authority which by law a parent of a child has in relation to the child and his property' (Children Act 1989).

The significance of this becomes quickly apparent when you consider that more than one in three children is born outside marriage. The issues of parental responsibility and maintenance are separate. An unmarried dad who doesn't have parental responsibility still has a duty to provide child support (see chapter 9).

Also a biological father still has some rights without parental responsibility - for example, to have contact with his children as well as being able to make an application for court orders relating to arrangements concerning the children (known as section 8 orders and covered in chapter 9).

Who has parental responsibility – you or your partner?

It depends. Mothers automatically have parental responsibility. Married fathers automatically do too and do not lose it on divorce. By contrast, unmarried fathers don't have automatic parental responsibility but may obtain it. There are a number of options open to them - they can:

- marry the mother;
- have their name registered on the birth certificate;
- enter into a parental responsibility agreement with the mother;
- make an application to the court for a parental responsibility order;
- obtain a residence order from the court; or
- become the child's guardian (see chapter 9).

As of December 2003, unmarried fathers have automatic parental responsibility for their children if they are registered as father on the birth certificate. The unmarried father can obtain parental responsibility by re-registering the birth certificate and including his name in the father section. If his name was registered on the birth certificate before December 2003, this will not automatically give him parental responsibility; he will have to obtain either the mother's consent, via a parental responsibility agreement, or the court's consent, via a parental responsibility order.

A parental responsibility agreement is an arrangement made by the mother and the unmarried father that places you, as unmarried parents, in the same position legally as married parents – in other words, the parents have agreed to share parental responsibility. If it is to be legally binding, the agreement must be made on a court form, signed and witnessed by court staff and be filed at the court. An application for a parental responsibility order may be made to the family proceedings court, the county court or the High Court. Forms are available at the court service website.

A parental responsibility order is a court order which only unmarried fathers can apply for if it is not possible to make an agreement with the child's mother. It is fairly uncommon for a father's application to be refused. The court will basically look at the father's commitment to the child and the attachment between child and father. If granted, a parental responsibility order puts the unmarried father in the same legal position as a married father in that he shares parental responsibility for the child with the mother. However, unlike a married father, in exceptional circumstances parental responsibility can be taken away from the unmarried father.

Can people other than you, the parents, acquire parental responsibility?

It is not acquired automatically by non-parents (e.g. carers such as grandparents, new partners, step-parents, etc.) even if they care for and are responsible on a day-to-day basis for the child. However, there are several ways to obtain it – by being appointed as guardian for the child if those with parental responsibility have died, by obtaining a residence order or by gaining a special guardianship order from the court, or by adopting the child.

Local authorities will be given parental responsibility if they are granted a care order for the child (see chapter 7). If this happens, the parents' parental responsibility is not lost but the local authority and parents 'share' parental responsibility. Although it is 'shared', if a care order is in place, the local authority can exercise its parental responsibility over and above that of the parents.

A special guardian will also have parental responsibility. The parental responsibility given to special guardians can be exercised to the exclusion of the birth parents. (For a more detailed discussion of special guardians, see chapter 9.) Also when a child is adopted the parental responsibility of the birth parents is extinguished (see chapter 2). Where a grandparent acquires parental responsibility because a residence order is in place, they share it with the parents.

What happens if ...

... you're expecting a baby, and have split from your partner, who wants to come to all your scans because he has 'father's rights'. Can he come?

It's up to you and the kind of relationship you want to foster with your ex. Strictly speaking, your baby isn't a legal person until birth and no one has parental responsibility. If your ex becomes a nuisance and tries to accompany you against your wishes, you should consider calling the police. Once your baby is born, you will have parental responsibility but your ex won't because you are unmarried.

... you are the father of a five-year-old with asthma and you'd like to know more but your ex says that it is none of your business. You were never married. Can you ask to see your son's medical records?

If you don't share parental responsibility, you have no legal right to see your son's records nor are the doctors under any obligation to discuss his condition. You could consider an application for a parental responsibility order and/or a specific issue order. If you are granted a parental responsibility order, it should enable you to request information about your son's health and then the specific issue order, hopefully, would not be required. A specific issue order could be used where there is a dispute with the mother about whether to share information, follow a prescribed course of treatment or where the matter is urgent. This is an application under the Children Act 1989, section 8 (there is more detailed discussion about section 8 orders in chapter 9).

... you aren't married to the mother of your children but your name is on their birth certificates. She says you don't have any rights. Is that true?

No, if your name was placed on the child's birth certificate after December 2003 you will automatically have parental responsibility for the child. Otherwise as an unmarried father, you do not have any automatic parental responsibility – you have to acquire it, see above.

... your ex-wife has decided to marry her new partner. If he gets parental responsibility, do you lose yours?

No. You will retain your parental responsibility despite the divorce and even if your ex-wife's husband is granted parental responsibility, it would not affect your responsibilities towards your child. Also, your ex-wife's new husband does not acquire parental responsibility just because he marries your ex-wife. Since December 2005, a step-parent has been able to acquire parental responsibility through a parental responsibility agreement or by obtaining a court order. A parental responsibility agreement would require both your and your ex's consent; otherwise, if that isn't possible, the step-parent could apply to court for an order, or make a joint application with your ex-wife for a residence order.

... your ten-year-old niece has lived with you and your partner for six months. You are concerned that you have no legal authority to sign for school trips and take her to the doctors, etc. Someone has told you to apply for parental responsibility. Are they right?

No, you've been misled. The only category of person who may apply for parental responsibility is the unmarried father. You can ask the court's permission to apply for a residence order and if successful parental responsibility would be awarded for the duration of the order.

You should also note that under the Children Act, you may act as 'a reasonable parent' would in the same circumstances. Effectively, the law allows people with care of children to act as reasonable parents to ensure a child's well-being or safety is not jeopardised because they do not have parental responsibility.

When does parental responsibility end?

For parents parental responsibility ends when your child reaches adulthood (in other words when they reach 18) or sooner if they marry or are adopted (where parental responsibility is effectively extinguished for birth parents and moves to the adoptive parents - see chapter 2). For non-parents, where parental responsibility has been acquired via a residence order, it ends when the order ends, usually at the age of 16 unless otherwise specified. However, if a father has obtained parental responsibility by virtue of a residence order, his parental responsibility for the child will go on longer than the residence order (i.e. to 18 years).

Again, if the father who was married to the mother when the child was born subsequently divorces her, he does not lose parental responsibility. Only when adoption takes place, can a mother lose parental responsibility. Parental responsibility diminishes as the child gets older and when a young person reaches 16/17 years old, parents have little say over the child's life.

Can you change your child's surname?

Only if all those with parental responsibility agree; if they don't, the parent seeking to change the name needs to obtain a court order.

A parent is able to change a child's name by 'a deed of change of name' (in other words, a deed poll) providing all those with parental responsibility agree. This does not mean that the birth certificate will change (that is considered to be a historical record). So if your child is asked for proof of identity and they have changed their name by deed poll they will have to show their birth certificate and deed poll. Once an application for a deed poll certificate has been completed all the official documents and records can be changed to the new name. To change the name on official documents and records, the deed poll document will need to be shown as evidence of the name change. If parents are in dispute about changing the child's surname, one parent can make an application to the court for an order. During this process both parents will be able explain their reasons for wanting to change their child's surname and a judge will ultimately make a decision for them.

If you discover that your ex is proposing to change your child's name and you do not have parental responsibility, you can seek a prohibited steps order (a section 8 order by the court preventing a parent doing a specific thing - see chapter 9).

If you were not married at the time the child's birth was registered, the child's surname can be changed from the mother's to the father's, if both parents agree. The birth can be re-registered and a new certificate issued (this will not of itself give parental responsibility, though).

If you aren't living with your child's other parent, can you take your child abroad on holiday?

It always makes sense to ensure that the other parent is happy for you to take the child abroad. Any person in whose favour a residence order has been made can remove a child from the country for up to one month without the consent of any other parental responsibility holders. If the proposed removal is for more than one month, the person with the residence order must secure permission in writing from everyone with parental responsibility or have permission of the court.

If the parent with whom the child lives does not have a residence order, they can take the child on holiday but should inform the non-resident parent of their holiday plans. From a strict legal point of view, they should get the written consent of all those with parental responsibility or this could amount to 'child abduction' under the law. If the non-resident parent objects, you will need to apply for a court order. If consent is not given freely or permission by the court granted, the parent who did not consent can involve an organisation like Reunite (which offers advice on child abduction) to have the child returned under the Hague Convention. Reunite has a child abduction prevention guide. That said, in practice often nothing comes of a child being taken without consent for less than one month and nothing will happen unless someone puts in a complaint that the child was taken without consent. A non-resident parent who wishes to take their child on holiday abroad generally has to negotiate this with the resident parent.

What if you cannot agree on a major decision about your child?

You could try family mediation. The aim of mediation is to take away the acrimony and resolve differences amicably. Mediation works in different ways in different parts of the country. Sometimes parents are seen separately and then are brought together to see if they can achieve a compromise solution. In other mediation services parents are seen together sometimes with a solicitor or a representative.

If the decision is something that cannot be resolved, then the parents can apply to the court for a specific issue order (see chapter 9 and information on section 8 orders). The parent does not have to have parental responsibility to be able to do this.

What about caring for your children's children? What rights do grandparents have?

The law doesn't give grandparents automatic rights to see their grandchildren, still less, look after them. The Grandparents Association estimates that as many as one million grandchildren are not allowed to see grandparents in the UK. Unlike estranged parents, who have a right to go to the courts to seek contact with their children, grandparents have to seek permission from the court before they can apply for contact. See chapter 9 for a discussion of grandparent contact issues.

It is reckoned an estimated 200,000 grandparents provide sole care for their children's children with little or no state support. However, it is often the case that grandparents have little choice but to care for children in the aftermath of a family catastrophe such as a death, divorce or drink and drug problems. More than other family members they are the ones left holding the baby.

As said before, grandparents, even when actually bringing up their grandchildren, do not automatically have parental responsibility. Nevertheless, while the grandchildren are living with them, grandparents are entitled to do 'what is reasonable in all the circumstances of the case for the purpose of safeguarding or promoting the child's welfare' under the Children Act – as are other non-parent carers such as step-parents. Basically this means that grandparents can take the day-to-day decisions (e.g. consenting to urgent medical treatment) which are reasonable for safeguarding the child's welfare despite not having parental responsibility.

The Grandparents Association notes that 'in theory' grandparents looking after their grandchildren have all the necessary day-to-day powers to make those decisions necessary for the normal upbringing of a child. However, they advise, even where there is no dispute between a parent and grandparent, and the grandparent is effectively bringing up the child, it is desirable to seek to obtain a residence order giving them parental responsibility.

It has been estimated that Britain's 14 million grandparents are supporting families by providing childcare worth £3.9 billion every year (Grandparents Plus, 2009). Grandparents' contributions to the economy was acknowledged in the 2009 budget when it was announced that grandparents who choose to give up work to provide childcare would no longer miss out on National Insurance Contributions and so could qualify for a full basic state pension. Grandparents Plus is campaigning for two weeks of 'granny leave' after the birth of a grandchild, plus flexible working arrangements and tax breaks.

There is little support for you as grandparents looking after your children's children or, indeed, for other family carers.

As for state support, only foster carers are entitled to support (see chapter 2). Grandparents might otherwise have a residence order, special guardianship order or no order at all (see chapter 9) and any allowance or support is entirely discretionary. According to the Family Rights Group, it is 'a real postcode lottery' and most grandparents receive nothing.

What if you are a step-parent – how do you acquire parental responsibility?

The marriage counselling service Relate reckons one in three people in the UK is likely to be involved in a step-family at some point in their life. You can only get parental responsibility for your partner's children by applying to court for a residence order. Married step-parents, as well as gay and lesbian step-parents who have entered into a civil partnership, are able to make a parental responsibility agreement or apply to a court for parental responsibility instead.

The lack of standing in law might well suit you if you are living with your partner's children because you feel that the absence of automatic legal or financial obligations is appropriate.

That said, Relate points out that 'the conflicts that arise from taking on emotional and financial responsibilities for children while having no rights over them comes up again and again in the difficulties experienced by all members of restructured families' (*Stepfathers*, Suzie Hayman, Relate, 2001).

Step-parents can put their relationship with their partner's children on a legal footing through adoption or applying for an order. Adoption by step-parents is quite unusual and only granted in exceptional circumstances. Acquiring parental responsibility does not mean that children are automatically acknowledged under the law as 'your children'. For example, if you die without a will your own children will inherit. If you want a stepchild to inherit, you have to specify this in a properly drawn up will. See chapter 9 for a discussion on the intestacy rules.

Children

What does it mean to be a child under the law?

By law, your children do not reach full legal independence until their 18th birthday although the ages at which your children can take part in what might be considered grown-up activities vary widely – for example, the right to sign up and join the army (or, for that matter, the right to buy a packet of cigarettes) is 16 years. We consider how the law treats children as they grow into young adults over chapters 6 and 7.

There is a body of domestic and international law that has evolved which aims to protect children from harm and to provide for their needs.

In recent years, there has been a shift in legal culture insofar as children have increasingly been recognised as having rights to have their own voices heard. As mentioned earlier in this chapter, that is the principle that is enshrined in the 1989 Children Act.

Children's wishes and feelings – as far as they can be ascertained – are factors that courts must take into account when reaching a decision about the child's welfare. However, the mechanism for determining children's wishes and feelings is far from perfect and there is much debate about how this could be improved, including whether judges should meet with the children concerned.

Children have their own human rights treaty – the UN Convention on the Rights of the Child (CRC). This was signed in 1989 and ratified by the UK in 1991, and covers every aspect of children's lives. It includes some rights which are also protected under the European Convention on Human

Rights (ECHR), such as the right to life, the right to respect for privacy, and the right to freedom of expression.

Anyone in the UK can take individual complaints about violations of their ECHR rights to the European Court of Human Rights in Strasbourg. Since 2000, when the ECHR was made part of UK domestic law by the Human Rights Act, people can also raise these complaints in the UK courts.

By contrast, there is no international court that will hear individual complaints about violations of children's rights under the CRC and, as the CRC has not been incorporated into our domestic law, such complaints cannot be raised in their own right in the UK courts. However, because the UK has ratified the CRC, it is obliged under the international law of treaties to comply with it. This means, for example, that if a child brings a claim in the domestic courts about a breach of their ECHR rights, the court should consider related provisions of the CRC when interpreting the child's ECHR rights.

In addition to the CRC rights reflected in the Human Rights Act, there are many rights which go further – recognising children's evolving capacities, as well as their vulnerability. For example, the treaty protects a child's right to have their best interests made a primary consideration in all matters affecting them (Article 3). Also, there is protection for a child's right to participate in decision-making about matters that affect them, with due weight to be given to their wishes and feelings taking into account their age and maturity (Article 12).

Great importance is attached in the treaty to the role of parents as the main guardians of their children's rights, and the treaty enshrines a child's right not to be separated from their parents unless this is against their best interests. The treaty recognises the importance of both parents.

Groups that campaign to promote the welfare of children argue that the UK has a long way to go before children's rights under the CRC will be properly reflected. So organisations like the Children's Rights Alliance for England (CRAE) are seeking its incorporation into UK law for this purpose.

Children's rights – how does the country hold up?

In 2008, a report by the Children's Rights Alliance for England (CRAE) endorsed by 102 NGOs made 152 recommendations for improvements in the implementation of the CRC – 100 were described as requiring 'urgent action'. The CRAE is calling for the full implementation of the CRC.

The CRAE publishes an annual report on the state of children's rights in England to show key developments in children's human rights over the previous 12 months.

CRAE recommendations covered a wide range of areas and included:

- protection from age discrimination under the forthcoming Equality Bill;

- protection from electronic devices (called 'Mosquitoes') that emit high-pitched noise specifically designed to disperse young people;

- entitlement, if born out of wedlock to a British father, to register as a British citizen;

- the right to vote and to stand in public elections from the age of 16 years;

- the right to access information about their origins, the existence of any siblings and their extended family for children separated from their biological parents;

- the right to opt in or opt out of religious worship for children of sufficient understanding;

- stronger protection for babies and children affected by reality television programmes;

- a ban on all corporal punishment;

- a ban on all other cruel or degrading forms of punishment in private foster care, young offender institutions, secure training centres and military establishments;

- a legal presumption that siblings in care will be placed together unless it is not in their best interests.

The 2005 CRAE report recorded the following sobering statistics:	
Child homicides in 2003/04	**70**
Baby homicides in 2003/04	**27**
Child death in penal custody since 1990	**29**
Average weekly education in prison custody for 15- to 17-year-olds	**8 hours**
Child pedestrian and cycling deaths in 2004	**106**
Life expectancy of girl, Kensington and Chelsea	**85.8 years**
Life expectancy of boy, Manchester	**72.3 years**
Permanent exclusions from school in 2003/04	**9,880**
Asylum-seeking children detained each year	**2,000**

CONTACTS

For information about the law as it relates to children, as well as parents' rights and responsibilities, see the Children's Legal Centre (www.childrenslegalcentre.com) and Lawyers for Young People (www.lfyp.org.uk). For information on grandparents' rights, see www.grandparents-association.org.uk. To find out more about the law on child abduction, see www.reunite.org.

For information about the rights of children, see the Children's Rights Alliance for England (www.crae.org.uk). For court forms relating to parental responsibility, see the court service website (www.hmcourts-service.gov.uk).

CHAPTER TWO

Expectant parents

This chapter looks at those concerns facing expectant parents looking forward to the birth of their child. It is an exciting time in a couple's life and, for first-time parents, a precursor to a huge upheaval in their life. The chapter falls into five sections:

1. **Expecting the birth:** This first section begins by considering where you might choose to have your baby: hospital, home or maternity unit; the standard of antenatal care you can expect; as well as your right to determine the way in which you go into labour and get access to pain relief.

2. **After the birth:** Next we consider issues that might arise in the immediate aftermath of your new arrival; for example, the level of post-natal care you should expect and how you can register the birth of your child. This section also considers the right of young mothers to breastfeed in public and whether children have to have their jabs. Finally, this section considers your position should something go wrong in the hospital and the responsibility owed by healthcare professionals to you and your child. In particular, it considers how the law of negligence applies to mother and baby.

3. **Pregnancy and work:** This section looks at how starting a family affects the rights of you (and your partner) in the workplace. First, we consider at what point you should tell your employer that you are pregnant and your right to take time off for antenatal appointments. We then look at how your pregnancy might affect you in the workplace, how much time you can take off work to have your baby

and your pay during maternity leave. It then considers your return to your job after maternity leave, your rights to keep the same job on that return and whether you can change your hours to spend more time looking after your child. We also look at how becoming a mother might affect your career prospects. Finally, we look at fathers' rights and whether, if your partner is expecting a baby, you can you take time off.

4. **Other ways to start a family:** We consider here how couples begin families if there is a problem with fertility, such as donor insemination and surrogacy.

5. **Adoption and fostering:** We end the chapter with a discussion of adoption and fostering.

Expecting the birth

Where can you have your baby?

The vast majority of women give birth in hospital. You don't have to and there is no law forcing a woman to go to hospital to give birth. There are other options. Home births are increasingly popular and you might also opt for a birth centre or a midwife-led maternity unit, which is a halfway house between home and hospital and conventional consultant-led maternity units. Birth centres are not an option for everyone. Most only take women who have a high chance of delivering their baby normally. In addition, the government's policy, as outlined in a 2007 policy paper, is by the end of 2009 to promote choice in terms of options for a mother's place of birth and type of birth, such as to be able to offer all mothers the option of a home birth.

You want a home birth but your local health authority 'doesn't do' home births – do you have the right to insist?

Yes. You have a right but there is no absolute duty on the part of the health authority to provide support. Expectant mothers in the UK have a right to be attended by a midwife during birth with a corresponding obligation on the part of the local health authority to provide a midwife or doctor to attend the birth (under the NHS Acts 1946 and 1949). Recent government policies have pushed for pregnant women to have more continuity of care from midwives, so that they know their midwife and are able to plan what sort of birth they want, including providing care closer to where the woman lives.

Under the current law, the duty is to provide 'such facilities for the care of expectant and nursing mothers and young children as … are appropriate as part of the health service' (National Health Services Act 1977).

So women still have a right to a home birth – in other words, there are no laws forcing a woman to go to hospital to give birth (but there is no duty on the part of the health authority to provide support in general and a midwife in particular). If you refuse to go into hospital, then you cannot be compelled to go (there is an exception if you are deemed not to be mentally competent).

The government's policy is supportive of women who want a home birth. In early 2007, Patricia Hewitt, as Secretary of State for Health, promised every woman would be able to choose an attended home birth by the end of 2009. However, the availability of support is reckoned to be something of a postcode lottery and couples determined to have a home birth often face an uphill struggle. The support group the Association for Improvements in the Maternity Services (AIMS) notes 'as a result of this lack of clarity it is not uncommon for health trusts to suggest that if they are short of midwives around the time the woman goes into labour she will have to come to hospital, and many women then abandon their decision to birth at home'. It is good practice for there to be two midwives present for emergency purposes.

The group also notes that those women who are determined to give birth at home, and 'who make it absolutely clear (preferably in writing)' that they have no intention of going in, are eventually provided with a midwife. The midwife has a professional responsibility to the mother. This was clarified by the Nursing and Midwifery Council, which issued a circular stating that its professional standards 'require them to be competent to support women to give birth normally in a variety of settings including in the home'. If a woman telephones a midwife to say that she requires her services, the midwife cannot refuse to go.

It is perfectly legal to give birth alone, unassisted – in other words, with no midwife (whether this is accidental or deliberate). However, it is illegal for anyone other than a registered midwife or doctor or registered medical practitioner (or student of either) to 'attend' (take responsibility for care) a woman in labour except in an emergency. In other words, if your birth partner intended to act as a midwife they could be prosecuted. You would not be prosecuted. In one case where there was a successful prosecution, the baby's father had told the health authorities that he intended to act as a midwife for the birth. His wife had promised never to enter the hospital again because of poor treatment when having her first baby. The father was fined £500, which was paid by a sympathetic doctor (a member of AIMS). Since that time the group has challenged hospitals that threaten prosecution arguing that the law is intended to prosecute someone who is claiming to be a midwife when they do not have the qualifications (and not intended to prosecute partners, friends or relatives who offer to support the woman).

The Royal College of Midwives (RCM) does not support free birth and believes that an unsupported birth without a midwife will place a woman and her baby at risk. The RCM is concerned that the mother or child might be at risk if there was a deviation from a normal pregnancy, or a problem that the woman could not deal with.

As a result of the Nursing and Midwifery Council, the RCM and AIMS' lobbying, Jacqui Smith MP, the then minister of state at the Department of Health, clarified the position in 2002. She said that 'attending a woman in childbirth', as opposed to general support given by partners and relatives, 'has been an offence against the protected function of midwifery since the Midwives Act 1902 and the fines are set at a level to reflect the seriousness of the offence' ... 'By "attend" we mean, "assume responsibility for care" and this is not intended to outlaw husbands, partners and relatives whose presence and support during childbirth are extremely important.'

Can you be forced to attend hospital?

No, a mentally competent pregnant woman cannot be forced to go to a hospital, or accept treatment, against her will. One landmark case in 1998 concerned a woman who was sectioned under the Mental Health Act and then subjected to a forced caesarean for pre-eclampsia (a potentially life-threatening disorder that occurs only during pregnancy), which following subsequent examination of the notes she did not have. Her doctors obtained a court injunction to dispense with the need for her to consent to treatment. The judge who issued the order did not ask whether she was mentally competent, but simply granted the request. She was competent and disagreed with the treatment. She was not legally represented when her doctors sought the order, nor was she even informed that they were seeking one. Instead, she was detained in a mental health hospital and did not receive any treatment for the alleged pre-eclampsia, which the staff claimed was at a very dangerous stage. The Court of Appeal later awarded her damages for false imprisonment and trespass to the person. The Appeal judges reaffirmed the absolute right of a competent adult to refuse medical intervention, even if the result would mean that she or her baby died. A foetus has no legal status and therefore you cannot force a competent woman to undergo care in the interests of the 'baby'.

What level of antenatal care should you expect?

As part of NHS care, you should be offered a programme of antenatal care and a series of appointments to check on your health and that of the baby. These are usually undertaken by the midwife and occasionally the GP. Your first point of contact following your pregnancy should be with your midwife, who will discuss your options. According to the National Institute for Health and Clinical Excellence (NICE) (March 2008), if you are expecting your first child, you are likely to have up to ten appointments and if you have had a baby previously, then you should have around seven appointments. You can always ask for more for any reason, including particular concerns about the baby's health. The aim of these appointments is to check on you and your baby's progress. The first should be as early in the pregnancy as possible where you will receive information about (amongst other things) the antenatal screening options, dietary and exercise advice and stopping smoking. Before any test is done you should be given the reason for the test. The NICE guidance says that, 'your midwife or doctor should explain to you that decisions on whether to have tests rests with you, and they should make sure that you understand what those decisions will mean for you and your baby'.

The more thorough antenatal appointment is called the 'booking appointment', which ideally takes place by ten weeks and is more detailed and you will be asked about your medical, social and family history to determine what sort of care you will receive. You will also be weighed and measured. It is an opportunity to discuss options for your maternity care and the birth of your baby. You will be offered a series of tests, including an ultrasound scan, usually given between 10 and 14 weeks to estimate when your baby is due. It may also be part of a screening test for Down's syndrome. You should be offered another scan normally between 18 weeks and 21 weeks to check for any problems (an anomaly scan). Again, you have the right to choose which tests you want. Results from all tests will help the antenatal team and you to plan the best care.

Antenatal classes are there to help you and your partner prepare for labour, birth and early parenthood. There is a variety of options within the NHS and the private sector for both pregnant women and partners. Private providers such as the NCT, formerly the National Childbirth Trust, also provide antenatal classes. All NCT teachers take a three-year training course leading to a diploma in higher education.

Don't expect to see an obstetrician during the course of your pregnancy, unless there is a problem. If you want to see the obstetrician, you can. But unless there are any problems you will only see a midwife. Midwives have a responsibility to identify when things are going wrong and refer when necessary to the obstetrician.

What are your options when it comes to the birth itself?

You need to set out what you wish for your birth and pregnancy and plan accordingly. A midwife cannot carry out a procedure without a woman's consent and if a vaginal examination is an issue, then the midwife must respect this. Most maternity units will attempt to provide you with the sort of birth that you want but discuss with your midwife what local facilities and protocols there are. Check, for example, if it is possible to have access to a birthing pool and make clear if you want an active birth (where you have the freedom to move about). Most hospitals have birthing pools, and you can request one when you are in labour, which you should be able to get subject to availability. Generally speaking, you cannot book them in advance. If you're planning a home birth, you need to provide your own pool.

Your midwife will discuss all pain relief options with you – for example, Entonox (or 'gas and air') and an epidural, which is administered by a needle at the base of your spine. If you know you want an epidural, it is important to make that clear. You do not have a 'right' to one, though.

After the birth

What post-natal care should you expect?

NICE outlines the kind of care that women and their baby should expect in the first six to eight weeks after birth in its 2006 guidance. 'All healthcare professionals should treat you and your baby with respect, dignity, kindness and understanding and explain your care simply and clearly,' it says. NICE also points out that you should be provided with a personal child health record for your baby which should be kept by you and used to note your baby's health until they are at least five years old. It should be regularly updated. The NICE guidance says that in the first 24 hours after giving birth you should be offered 'privacy, adequate rest and be able to have food and drink whenever you need it and the healthcare professional should work with you to develop a written postnatal care plan'. This should include a record of the care you and your baby receive and will be filled in during every contact you have with a member of the healthcare team. Also in the first 24 hours, you should expect a number of health checks, from measuring blood pressure to offering to give your baby an injection of vitamin K (to prevent a rare but serious blood disorder). NICE recommends the injection is the best method to give your baby vitamin K but you should also be offered it in liquid form. This has to be given several times in the first two weeks. The midwife will come to your home to recommend that the baby is screened for potentially serious diseases. The midwife has responsibility for the first 28 days after birth of the care of mother and baby. In practice they visit your home for two weeks and then invite you to the clinic.

How do you register the birth?

It is a legal requirement to register the birth within 42 days (under the Births and Deaths Registration Act 1953). As to who should go to make the registration depends on whether you are married at the time of the birth or conception. If you are, then either one of you can register. If you aren't, then who goes depends on whether:

- you as a couple want the father's details to be entered in the register, then you can both go and sign the register together;

- the father is able to go; if not, but you want the father's details included, he can make a statutory declaration acknowledging paternity;

- the mother is able to go; if not, she may make a statutory declaration acknowledging the father's paternity on the same form as above; or

- there is a parental responsibility agreement in force (see chapter 1) or either parent has obtained an appropriate court order, then this document can be presented at the time of registration by either parent.

If the father's particulars are not recorded in the birth register, it may be possible for the birth to be re-registered to include his details at a later date. For information on registering a birth, see the General Register Office website (www.gro.gov.uk).

Do you have a right to breastfeed in public?

Not yet; however, if the Equality Bill (at the time of publication going through Parliament) becomes law, then mothers in England and Wales will have the right to breastfeed their babies in public. In Scotland, mothers already have this right and anyone who prevents a woman from doing so anywhere in public can be fined £2,000.

Breastfeeding in public in England and Wales is not illegal now, although according to the National Childbirth Trust 13 per cent of women in England and 16 per cent in Wales have been asked to stop, or made to feel uncomfortable when breastfeeding in a public place.

According to the Equality Bill, mothers have to be confident that they can feed their babies in a cafe, restaurant or shop 'without the embarrassment of having the owner to ask them to stop' ... 'This type of discrimination has been unlawful for women with babies of any age for more than 30 years, and a mother could challenge the owner under the Sex Discrimination Act.' That Act was strengthened by the government in 2008 so that if the baby was younger than six months the mother could also challenge the owner on grounds of her maternity. The Equality Bill published in April 2009 promised to 'make it clear that it is unlawful to force breast-feeding mothers and babies out of places like these shops, public galleries and restaurants'.

Do your children have to have their jabs?

No. In the UK, vaccination is a matter of parental discretion. It was reported in 2008 that only 85 per cent of children received the controversial MMR (measles, mumps and rubella) jab; however, it dropped to as low as 80 per cent after furore over the safety of the vaccine. Fears linking MMR to autism led to parents not arranging for their children to receive immunisations. The Department of Health argues that experts from around the world have found 'no credible scientific evidence for such a link and there is now a large amount of evidence showing that there is no link'. In France, all children have to have the full set of jabs before they can go to school. A similar requirement to demand proof that pupils have had a full range of jabs, including MMR, before allowing them to register was flagged up by New Labour in 2008; however, the British Medical Association labelled it 'Stalinist' and counterproductive. The NHS has a dedicated immunisation website.

What happens if something goes wrong in the hospital?

If something goes wrong in connection with the birth of your child, first you need to seek an explanation from those responsible. If that fails, then it is important that you make a complaint in writing to the complaints manager at the NHS Trust, Strategic Health Authority (SHA) or Primary Care Trust (PCT). If you are unhappy, you can then take your complaint to independent review. If you are still dissatisfied after the complaints procedure has been completed, you can ask the Health Service Commissioner (the Ombudsman) to investigate. The complaints procedure is slightly different in the private sector (some private hospitals have their own complaints system and their complaints policy can be found on their website).

Every doctor owes a duty of care to a patient irrespective of whether that patient is in the NHS or private sector. If you believe that you have been the victim of an accident in a hospital, then you, as claimant, can bring your claim in negligence. If you have paid for your treatment, then you can bring two claims – one for breach of contract (under the law of contract) and the second for the negligent act or omission (in tort). The burden of proving a claim is on you as claimant. Your case will fail unless you can show that on the balance of probabilities (in other words, that it was more likely than not) your injury was caused by the negligence of the doctor as opposed to some other innocent cause.

For you to succeed, you must prove that:

- the doctor owed you a duty of care (such a duty has been established in case law as well as under NHS legislation);

- there was a breach of that duty because the doctor failed to reach the standard of practice required by law;

- there was an adverse outcome resulting in an injury; and

- the breach of the duty caused, or contributed significantly, to the injury or damage.

Only if the court is satisfied that all issues have been proved on the balance of probabilities will you succeed in your claim against the defendant whether it is an NHS Trust, SHA, PCT or private healthcare professional.

There is a time limit under which a claim can be brought (under the Limitation Act 1980 and known as the 'limitation period'). An adult generally has three years from the date of the alleged incident, or three years from the date of knowledge if later, to begin the action. By contrast, a child's limitation period does not begin to run until his 18th birthday, after which he has three years in which to issue proceedings. The limitation period of an individual of any age who is incapable of understanding does not begin to run until he regains capacity or dies. If the 'patient' dies, then his personal representative has three years to bring a claim on behalf of the dead person's estate.

How does the law of negligence apply to a mother and her baby?

An unborn baby has no legal personality – in other words, it is not regarded as a person in the eyes of the law. At birth, a baby can bring a claim for injury suffered pre-natally provided it is born alive. The baby through a 'litigation friend' (in other words, someone deemed under the law competent to bring the claim and usually but not always the baby's mother in this context) can pursue a claim for negligence against a doctor for injuries suffered as a result of pre-birth negligence (under the Congenital Disabilities (Civil Liability) Act 1976).

That legislation does not enable the baby to sue his own mother for any actions taken by her while in the womb which caused harm. So a baby cannot sue his mother for smoking, drinking, taking drugs, or refusing treatments (e.g. a caesarean section). One exception to this rule is that a baby can sue his mother if born with disabilities if she was pregnant (or ought reasonably to have known that she was) and failed to take reasonable care while driving a motor vehicle. In such a case, the baby sues the mother's insurance company, and not the mother directly to avoid conflict. A baby born disabled, as a result of fertility treatment, has the right to bring an action against a person for the damage resulting from a wrongful act – for example, failure to carry out proper tests on the embryo and failing to diagnose a birth defect (under the 1976 Act, as amended by the Human Fertilisation and Embryology Act 1990).

The 1976 Act enables a baby, once born alive, to sue for damages any person who has caused him to be born disabled by that person's alleged wrongful act. But, as legal attempts against the makers of the MMR vaccination have shown, proving causation in brain damage cases is particularly difficult. Under the 1976 Act, a pregnant mother who is assaulted and as a consequence goes into premature labour must show that her live infant's disabilities were caused by the assault. But the assailant may be prosecuted for homicide if his unlawful act causes death, after birth, of a baby who is born alive. In criminal cases, the law treats the foetus as part of the mother, and thus injury to mother and foetus is unlawful.

It is possible for a mother who has reckless disregard for an unborn child by, say, smoking, drinking or taking drugs to be liable for wilful destruction of a foetus capable of being born alive (under the Infant Life

Preservation Act 1929); however, it is doubtful that she would have the necessary 'intent' to be found guilty. She could also be liable for prosecution under the same legislation if she deliberately caused herself to miscarry, or knowingly did something that was virtually certain to cause her to miscarry or brought about the death of a foetus which was capable of being born alive (again, the requirement of 'virtual certainty' means that criminal prosecution is unlikely).

Pregnancy and work

You're pregnant. Should you tell your boss straight away? How long can you leave it?

The law goes to considerable lengths to protect both the safety and well-being of pregnant mothers, and their careers. Fathers are also allowed to take time off work to spend time with their new family.

Ideally, you should tell your employer you are pregnant at the earliest opportunity. Employers have a duty, as soon as they know, to take special measures to protect your health. Most people wait until the 12th week of pregnancy and they have the scan confirming the pregnancy before telling friends and loved ones that they are expecting. If you have particular concerns (e.g. you might work with powerful chemicals), you can always tell your employer confidentially.

You must tell your employer you are pregnant by the end of the 15th week before the expected week of childbirth (about the 25th week of pregnancy). At this point you will need to tell the employer the date the baby is due and choose a date to start maternity leave (which can always be changed if you give 28 days' notice). If you don't tell your employer you are pregnant in time, you may lose some of your rights, including the right to paid maternity leave. This is also the latest date by which your partner or husband should inform their employer if they want to take statutory paternity leave.

Can you take time off for antenatal appointments?

You have a right to time off on full pay for check-ups. Your employer cannot unreasonably refuse you time off (but the law gives no guidance on what is reasonable). Your employer can refuse to give you time off (except on the first appointment) if you do not produce an appointment card and a medical certificate to prove that you are pregnant. The law is also unclear on whether antenatal care includes relaxation and 'parent-craft' classes but the government takes the view that these are included provided a doctor or midwife has recommended them. Your employer cannot insist that you make up the lost time, or rearrange your shifts so that the appointment now falls in non-working time.

Will you lose pay (or even your job) if pregnancy stops you working?

By law, your employer should already have carried out a workplace risk assessment including an assessment of any health and safety risks. Once you tell your employer you are pregnant, it must take steps to address any specific risks before you get to the stage where your job is causing you pain or health risks. This may include altering your existing duties or, if that is not possible, offering you another job which does not carry the same risks. The alternative job must be suitable in terms of your position, skill and experience, and the terms and conditions (including pay) must be the same as, or not significantly worse than, your current job. Even then, you have the right to refuse if you have good reason – for example, if it has different hours which you cannot reasonably fit in with your other commitments such as childcare. You have a right to go back to your old job when it is safe to do so.

Your employer cannot dismiss you for any pregnancy-related reason, even if you have to stop working altogether. If there is no suitable alternative work, the employer must suspend you, and must continue to pay you your normal salary, unless you have unreasonably refused a suitable alternative job.

If you are sick during your pregnancy, your employer's normal sick pay rules will apply. This means you may only receive statutory sick pay, unless your employer has a more generous policy. However, you must not be paid less than other sick employees, and your employer must not dismiss you for reasons that involve pregnancy-related sickness.

If you are not working (on either sick leave or suspension), your employer cannot make you use up your annual leave, or make you start your maternity leave early. However, your maternity leave will start automatically if you are absent for a pregnancy-related reason in the four weeks before the expected week of childbirth.

How much time can you take off work to have your baby?

The right to maternity leave and pay has steadily improved in recent years. The current law allows up to one year's maternity leave for all employees, regardless of length of service. This is split into 26 weeks' ordinary maternity leave followed by a further 26 weeks' additional maternity leave. You can take as much or as little of this leave entitlement as you like, although it is against the law to go back to work for at least two weeks after giving birth (four weeks if you work in a factory).

Will you get paid during maternity leave?

First, check your written employment contract or staff handbook (if there is one) to see if your employer has its own policy for pay which exceeds the requirement under statute. Otherwise, if you started working for your employer before the baby was conceived, and your average earnings are over the lower earnings limit for class 1 National Insurance Contributions (£95 a week for the 2009/10 tax year), you should qualify for statutory maternity pay (SMP). Average earnings are calculated based on your last eight weeks' earnings before the end of the 15th week before the expected week of childbirth. If you are paid monthly, this generally means your payslips for the fifth and sixth months of pregnancy, averaged out on a weekly basis. For weekly paid employees it will be the average of the last eight payslips before the end of the 15th week before the expected week of childbirth.

The first six weeks of SMP are paid at 90 per cent of your average earnings. The remainder is paid at a rate set by the government for the relevant tax year (£123.06 a week for 2009/10) or 90 per cent of your earnings if this is lower. If you receive a pay rise during maternity leave, your SMP will have to be increased accordingly. By a strange quirk of the law (beneficial from your point of view), your SMP has to be recalculated from day one, as if you had received the pay rise before the period on which your average earnings were based. You should therefore be entitled to a top-up payment for the SMP you have already received. SMP is paid for 39 weeks (nearly nine months), having increased from 26 weeks in April 2007. The government plans eventually to increase it to a year, although there is no date set for this to happen.

Will you be able to keep the same job on your return from maternity leave?

Generally, you are entitled to return to the job you held before you went on leave. This means not only that the 'nature' of your job as defined in your contract must be the same, but also that you must be employed in the same capacity and place as before, even if your employer has the power under your contract to move you to different roles or even offices. The aim of the law here is to ensure that your return to work involves the minimum disruption possible for you.

If you have taken more than six months' maternity leave, your employer may offer you a suitable alternative job, but only if it is not 'reasonably practicable' to offer you your old job. For example, it may have reorganised your department and some job descriptions may have changed.

Your terms and conditions in any case must also be no less favourable than they would have been if you had not been absent. Therefore, if your colleagues have all received a pay rise, you must also receive one.

How will becoming a mother affect your career prospects?

From a strict legal viewpoint, it shouldn't. Any negative treatment of a woman because she has become pregnant or had a child, including any disruption that inevitably goes with childbirth and maternity leave, is viewed under the law as a form of unlawful sex discrimination. There are laws to enable you to keep your old job and to take advantage of family-friendly working arrangements where possible (see elsewhere in this section). However, some mothers feel that their prospects for promotion are no longer what they were.

The reality is that, while some employers are committed to family-friendly working, others are less so, and the law can be expensive and time-consuming to enforce. Legal aid is not available in employment tribunal cases so, unless you can find a law centre or Citizens Advice Bureau to take on your case, you will have to pay a solicitor or go it alone. It can be very difficult to show that your lack of promotion or your meagre bonus is due to motherhood, or to challenge your employer's 'evidence' that someone else is a better performer than you. That is not to say that it is not possible. For information about sex discrimination and what you can do to prevent it, contact the Equality and Human Rights Commission.

Your partner is expecting a baby – can you take time off?

Statutory paternity leave is available to employees who have been employed for at least 26 weeks at the end of the 15th week before the expected week of childbirth. You must tell your employer that your partner is expecting a child (and when it is expected) at least by the end of that week. You can take either one or two consecutive weeks' leave, which can be taken immediately on the day your child is born, or at any time within eight weeks of the birth (or the expected week of childbirth, if the birth is early). Some employers will give you full pay but, if not, you have the right to statutory paternity pay. This is paid by your employer, at a rate set by the government each tax year (£123.06 per week for 2009/10), or 90 per cent of your average weekly earnings, whichever is the lower.

If two weeks is not enough, you may extend your paternity leave by taking paid annual leave (if your employer agrees) or by taking unpaid parental leave.

In 2011 the government plans to introduce up to 6 months' 'additional paternity leave', which will only be available if your partner goes back to work before the end of her maternity leave. So, for example, if she has taken 6 months of her 12 months' maternity leave, you will be entitled to take the remaining 6 months as additional paternity leave (of which the first 3 months would be paid at the statutory rate). If your partner has gone back to work after 9 months, you would be entitled to 3 months' unpaid leave.

Paternity leave is available not only to the biological father. If you are not the father but are married to the mother, in a civil partnership with her, or cohabiting with her in an 'enduring family relationship', and expect to be the main person (apart from the mother) responsible for the child's upbringing, you will also qualify. You may also take paternity leave if you are jointly adopting a child and your spouse, civil partner or cohabiting partner is taking adoption leave.

Other ways to start a family

Your partner is expecting a baby by donor insemination. What will your legal position be in relation to the child?

In the case of the many couples that cannot have a baby, the woman may be fertile and one way of achieving a pregnancy is artificial insemination (otherwise known as 'donor insemination'). As the number of babies available for adoption is limited (see later in this chapter), the treatment often offers the only chance of a family.

There are many centres throughout the UK licensed to provide treatment. The decision to go ahead with treatment is often difficult. There are many medical, ethical, religious and legal aspects that need to be considered. Donor insemination via licensed clinics is legal in this country and, provided it is carried out with the husband's consent, cannot provide grounds for divorce on the basis of unreasonable conduct.

Any woman carrying a baby is the legal mother. Her husband (or partner if unmarried) is the legal father as long as he consents to the treatment. However, where a couple is not married only the child's mother is automatically considered to have 'parental responsibility' – see chapter 1. The donor has no parental rights or legal obligations towards the child. However the child has the right, once they reach 18 years of age, to ask for details about the donor. They would have to apply to the Human Fertilisation and Embryology Authority to access this information, which is kept on a central register. It is the body that has powers under the law to license clinics, monitor their standards as well as recording information about donors, couples who are provided with treatment and children born as a result. Information held by the HFEA is kept strictly confidential.

There is no legal requirement to tell the child how they were conceived, although it is recommended that the child is told that they were conceived through the use of donated gametes (sperms and eggs). It is important where donor insemination is performed for a genetic reason that the child should know that they are not at risk from inherited disease.

In August 2009 (as a result of the Human Fertilisation and Embryology Act 2008) female civil partners who use fertility treatment to conceive a child are treated as married couples plus female couples not in a civil partnership but receiving fertility treatment may also be registered as parents in the same way as unmarried heterosexual couples. The new rules apply in respect of children conceived on or after 6 April 2009, not from August.

The law requires both the man who contributes the sperm and the woman who contributes the egg to give consent before the embryos are created and when they are implanted to try to produce a baby. Either can withdraw consent at any time. It is an issue that arose in the case of Natalie Evans, a woman who fought for five years to use the frozen embryos she created with her former fiancé. She was left infertile after being treated for ovarian cancer and had six eggs fertilised with the sperm of her then partner, Howard Johnston. He withdrew his consent for her to attempt conception with the embryos after the couple separated, prompting Evans to appeal through the courts and to the European Court of Human Rights. The Strasbourg court ruled against her.

If you become a sperm donor, will your anonymity be preserved?

New rules were introduced in 2005 to lift anonymity from sperm, egg and embryo donors and allow donor-conceived children to access the identity of their donor when they reach the age of 18. The change in law removed the discrepancy that existed between the rights of donor-conceived people and those of adopted people. A number of other countries already provide such people with access to information about their donor. The regulations broadly apply to people who register after 1 April 2005, and people who donated before that date would not be identifiable (there are transitional rules which mean some children conceived before April 2005 can have identifiable donors) but generally this means that the first time 18-year-olds will be able to ask for the identity of their donor – if they choose – will be in 2023.

What's the legal position concerning surrogacy?

Most couples that have problems having a child opt for hospital treatment, but for some no amount of medical treatment can help. These are couples where a woman cannot conceive because, for example, it is not medically safe for her to carry a baby and adoption might not be possible.

There are two types of surrogacy. 'Straight surrogacy' (also known as 'traditional surrogacy') involves the egg of the surrogate mother and the sperm of the intended father. Here the baby is biologically related to the intended father and the surrogate mother. 'Host surrogacy' (also known as 'gestational surrogacy') uses the egg of the intended mother or a donor egg combined with the sperm of her husband or donor sperm (but not where donor eggs have been used as well) and put into the surrogate mother. In this case an IVF clinic is always required. A baby conceived by this method has no biological connection to the surrogate mother. This is by far the more difficult way to get pregnant. The chances of it working are low and it takes a lot more time and energy to complete.

The positive aspects of surrogacy are that, if you are lucky enough to find a surrogate and everything goes according to plan, you have a child that is either your husband's or, as in host surrogacy, a child of you both. On the minus side, if the surrogate decides to keep the child she has a right to do so; the law states that she is the legal mother even in host surrogacy (but the question as to whether she could keep the baby is a complex legal one and there are some cases of the court awarding care to the commissioning parents notwithstanding the surrogate mother's status as the mother).

Any commercial aspect in a surrogacy is specifically banned under the law, although it is possible to cover a party's expenses. The Surrogacy

Arrangements Act 1985 makes it an offence for anyone who acts 'on a commercial basis if … any payment is at any time received by himself or another in respect of it'. But it also goes on to state 'payment' does not include payment to or for the benefit of a surrogate mother or prospective surrogate mother. It is illegal for a commercial agency to profit from brokering a surrogacy arrangement, but an offence for payments to pass between the surrogate and the intended parents. However, if the parents have paid more than 'reasonable expenses' they will have more difficulty getting the parental order to secure their position as the child's parents. In order to carry out a legal surrogacy in the UK you should apply for what is known as 'a parental order' (as distinct from a parental responsibility order). To be granted a parental order the intended parents must:

- be over 18;
- be married to one another (as of April 2010, unmarried and same sex couples will be able to apply);
- be domiciled in the UK (at least one of the applicants) ;
- be a biological parent to the child (at least one of the applicants) ;
- make the application within six months of the birth;
- have used artificial conception (i.e. not by sexual intercourse between the surrogate mother and intended father);
- consent (the surrogate mother, and her husband if she is married);
- have the child in their care at the time of the application; and
- have paid no more than reasonable expenses to the surrogate mother, unless authorised by the court.

Once the child is born the surrogate mother has sole parental rights over the child unless the father is named on the birth certificate or the surrogate mother enters into a parental responsibility agreement with the child's father (see chapter 1). This then gives the surrogate mother and the child's father equal rights over the child depending on the surrogate mother's marital status (in other words, if married, her husband will have parental responsibility).

The parental order can take from four months to a year to be granted. Someone from the court called a 'parental order reporter' will be assigned to your case who will visit both surrogate mother and couple separately and some weeks after the birth ask the surrogate mother if she is happy to relinquish all rights to the child. Once the order has been granted by the court all rights pass to the couple. A new birth certificate is then issued with the couple's names on.

Adoption and fostering

What is adoption?

It is a way of providing a new family for children who cannot be brought up by their own parents. It's a legal procedure in which parental responsibility (see chapter 1) is transferred to the adopters. Once an adoption order has been granted, it can't be reversed except in extremely rare circumstances. An adopted child loses all legal ties with their biological mother and father and becomes a full member of the new family usually taking the family's name.

Who can adopt?

You have to be over 21. There is no upper age limit. Any criminal record will need to be carefully looked into but, apart from some offences against children, will not necessarily rule someone out. Considerable effort is made to find a family that reflects the child's individual identity but that is not always achievable. Social workers will have to make a decision about when to consider alternative families in order to minimise delay for the child. Children would then be placed with families that best match their needs even if that means, for example, they are of a different ethnic group. A single person – heterosexual, lesbian or gay – can adopt. Since 30 December 2005 unmarried couples in England and Wales can apply to adopt jointly.

How do you apply to adopt?

You need to go through an agency. Some agencies, like Barnardo's, are voluntary adoption agencies but the majority are part of the local authority children's services. People are not limited to their own immediate locality but most agencies work roughly within a 50-mile radius of their office so social workers can easily visit.

It usually takes at least six months for social workers from an adoption agency to get to know prospective adopters, assess them and help prepare them for the task ahead. Confidential enquiries will be made of the local children's services and the police. Applicants will also need to see their GP for a medical examination and will be asked to provide personal references from at least two friends and one family reference.

The agency's independent adoption panel will consider a report on the application and recommend whether or not applicants are suitable to be approved as adopters. Prospective adopters will be given the opportunity to attend their approval panel.

If an agency is planning not to approve the prospective adopters, the applicants can make representations to the agency decision-maker asking them to review their determination or can apply to the Independent Review Mechanism for their application to be heard by an independent panel unconnected with their assessing agency.

An agency will try to match approved adopters with a child. It can also enquire about children being profiled in a number of family-finding publications, websites or in the local press. In England and Wales, agencies also refer prospective adopters to the Adoption Register for England and Wales, which links waiting children with approved prospective adopters. The proposed match will be presented to an adoption panel, which will recommend whether to proceed with the placement.

What happens when a child moves in with their new adoptive parents?

Before a child can move in, the placing authority must apply to the court for a placement order (this is its authority to place for adoption). Biological parents who do not agree with the adoption arrangements will be able to be heard at this point.

The child will move to live with their new parents after an introductory period lasting from a week to a month or two, depending on the child's age and needs. Social workers will remain involved to support the new family and the child at least until an adoption order is made.

There are certain minimum periods for which the child must live with the adopters before an adoption order can be made, or, in England and Wales, before an application can be made to the court. A birth mother cannot give consent to adoption until her child is at least six weeks old but she can agree to her child being placed for adoption before the child is six weeks old and will then need to consent once the child reaches six weeks of age. Whether birth parents do or do not agree with the plan for adoption, there is a process for the agreement to be independently witnessed. If birth parents do not agree to adoption, there are circumstances in which the court can override their wishes. In many cases the question of consent will be considered by the court before the child is placed for adoption. A children's guardian will be appointed by the court to investigate and give advice to the court on the child's best interests. In some circumstances, it will be necessary for the question of consent to be considered when the adopters actually apply for the final adoption order.

Do birth parents and other relatives have any contact with their child after adoption?

It is common for there to be an exchange of written information, perhaps once or twice a year, via the adoption agency. There will be unique arrangements for each individual child, which may mean direct contact for some children with various members of their birth family, including grandparents and brothers and sisters, who may be placed elsewhere. Sometimes there will also be contact with birth parents – if this is best for the child.

Do adopted children want to trace their birth parents?

Today, many children will know something of their origins and may have contact with birth relatives. Since 1975 adopted people in England and

Wales have had the right to see their original birth certificate when they reach the age of 18. Some people are satisfied with the fuller knowledge and understanding gained in this way, while others want to try to trace their birth parents or other family members. With access to the Internet, many agencies are finding that adopted adults and children are searching for birth family members independently.

What about adoption by step-parents?

Sometimes step-parents want to adopt the children from the previous relationship of their new partner. If this happens, the child's legal links with their absent birth parent and that parent's wider family will be broken. Alternative ways of settling the child's situation may be better for some children. The Adoption and Children Act 2002 introduced a special guardianship order, which confers parental responsibility (see chapter 9).

You are adopting a child – can you take time off?

Yes; parents who adopt have very similar rights to other parents when it comes to taking leave. Within seven days of being notified by an adoption agency that you have been matched with a child, you must tell your employer the date the child is expected to be placed in your care, the date you plan on starting your leave, and whether you will be taking adoption leave or paternity leave. Only one of you may take adoption leave; the other one may take paternity leave.

Statutory adoption leave, like statutory maternity leave, lasts up to one year. You may qualify for statutory adoption pay if you meet the minimum length of service and average earnings criteria. You must have been working for your employer for at least 26 weeks by the end of the week in which the agency notifies you of the match, and your average earnings must be over the lower earnings limit for class 1 National Insurance Contributions (£90 a week for the 2008/09 tax year).

Adoption leave and pay are only available if you are adopting a child through a UK adoption agency or an approved overseas agency. It is not available if you are adopting a stepchild or in other situations where no adoption agency is involved.

What is fostering?

It is a way of providing a family life for children who cannot live with their own parents. It is often used to provide temporary care while parents get help sorting out problems, take a break, or to help children or young people through a difficult period. Often children will return home once the problems have been resolved. Others stay in long-term or permanent foster care, some may be adopted, and others will move on to live independently.

Types of foster care include:

- **Emergency:** Where children need somewhere safe to stay for a few nights.

- **Short term:** Where carers look after children for a few weeks or months, while plans are made for the child's future.

- **Short breaks:** Where disabled children or children with special needs or behavioural difficulties enjoy a short stay on a pre-planned, regular basis with a new family, and their parents or usual foster carers have a short break for themselves.

- **Remand fostering:** Where young people are 'remanded' by the court to the care of a specially trained foster carer.

- **Long-term or permanent fostering:** Not all children in foster care want to be adopted, especially older children or those who continue to have regular contact with their relatives. These children live with long-term foster carers until they reach adulthood and are ready to live independently.

- **'Family and friends' or 'kinship' fostering:** Where children who are looked after by a local authority are cared for by people they already know within their family's extended network.

- **Private fostering:** Where the parents make an arrangement for the child to stay with someone else who is not a close relative and has no parental responsibilities and the child stays with that person for more than 27 days. However, parents and private foster carers have a legal responsibility to alert their local authority if this arrangement is in place.

All approved foster carers are registered with and contracted to a local authority or voluntary or independent fostering agency. The foster carer's role is to provide quality care for the child. All children in foster care will be looked after by a local authority and the foster carers will work in partnership with the local authority to provide this.

It is best for children to live with foster carers who reflect and understand the child's heritage, ethnic origin, culture and language, and fostering agencies need carers from all types of backgrounds. People do not need to be married to become a foster family – they can also be single, divorced or cohabiting. Gay men and lesbians can become foster carers, although in Scotland they can only do so as single individuals living on their own. There are no upper age limits for fostering, but fostering agencies expect people to be mature enough to work with the complex problems that children needing fostering are likely to have and be fit enough to perform a very demanding task.

What preparation do foster carers get?

If you want to become a foster carer, you need to go through thorough preparation and assessment. You also need to attend groups where you learn about the needs of children coming into foster care. Alongside this, you receive visits from a social worker. The social worker will then prepare an assessment report that is presented to an independent fostering panel, which recommends whether you can become a foster carer. All carers have an annual review and any training that's needed to ensure they are suitable to continue fostering. In April 2008, the Children's Workforce Development Council (CWDC) introduced new training standards for foster carers which new carers are expected to have met by the time of their first annual review. Some carers also take a national qualification such as an NVQ level 3 Caring for Children and Young People.

All foster carers receive an allowance to cover the cost of caring for a child in their home. For foster carers working on behalf of an agency, this is set by the individual fostering agency. Increasingly, fostering is being seen as a 'professional' role and many local authorities, voluntary and independent fostering agencies run schemes, which pay foster carers a fee.

How is fostering different from adoption?

Fostering is different from adoption because when a child is in foster care, the child's parents and/or the local authority still have legal responsibility for them. When a child is adopted, all legal responsibility for the child passes to the new family, as though the child had been born into that family, and the local authority and the birth parents no longer have formal responsibility for the child.

When there is no possibility for a child to return home to their parents, attempts will be made to see if anyone else in the family can care for them. If this is not possible, a family must be found who can provide permanence for the child, to allow them to feel as secure as possible. This happens through either long-term fostering or adoption.

If a foster carer decides that they want to adopt a child, they can ask to be assessed as a possible adopter for that child.

CONTACTS

For information for expectant parents, see the NCT (www.nct.org.uk) and for advice on MMR and the vaccines, see www.immunisation.nhs.uk/Vaccines/MMR. For information about the law on sex discrimination, see the Equality and Human Rights Commission (www.equalityhumanrights.com).

For information about adoption and fostering, see the British Association for Adoption & Fostering (www.baaf.org.uk).

CHAPTER 3
Early years

This chapter considers pre-school childcare. If you are a new parent planning to return to work, sooner or later you will need to think about childcare. There are a number of different options you might consider: childminder, nanny or nursery. Finally, we look at changing your hours at work so that you can spend more time with your children and the possibility of working flexitime.

You are thinking of returning to work and thinking of childcare – what are your options?

You might want to consider the following:

- **Childminders** are generally self-employed and work in their own homes caring for children. If they care for children under the age of eight years, they are required by law to be registered and inspected by Ofsted in England or by the Care and Social Services Inspectorate for Wales.

  Childminders are registered to look after a maximum of six children under eight years, including a maximum of three under-fives. These numbers include their own children. All childminders require introductory training, should have public liability insurance, a health check, and an enhanced Criminal Records Bureau (CRB) disclosure (see later), as well as a valid first-aid certificate.

  Childminders responsible for over-eight-year-olds do not have to be registered or inspected by the likes of Ofsted. However, like nannies, they can be approved under the government's Voluntary Childcare Register in England, and the Childcare Approval Scheme in Wales.

- **Nannies** work in your home caring for your children. Some live in, others come to work every day and others work for two or more families. Unlike childminders, nannies do not have to be registered and inspected. Many nannies are trained but there are no legal requirements for training, the number of children they look after, or for a CRB disclosure; however, they can now be approved under the Voluntary Childcare Register in England, and the Childcare Approval Scheme in Wales.

- **Nurseries** care for lots of children at once, usually of mixed ages. Several staff work in a nursery, and your child will usually have a 'key worker'. Nurseries tend to offer sociable environments with a broad range of activities for children.

There is a difference between childcarers who are required to be registered by law (including childminders caring for children under eight, nurseries and after-school clubs) and those who opt to become registered or approved. Those required by law to register will need to have a minimum of an enhanced CRB disclosure; first-aid training for people who work with children; introductory training; workplace training; and completed health declarations. Those who are permitted to voluntarily become registered will not need to meet all of these elements.

Anyone who cares for a child for more than two hours a day in a setting other than the child's home and for reward must be registered. In September 2009 Ofsted clarified this point and surprised many parents by reminding people that the requirement included those parents who regularly looked after their friends' children. The regulator stressed that people who babysit for one another's children for more than two hours at a time or on more than 14 days per year should be registered where parents receive a 'reward' for the childcare. Reward could include money or simply free babysitting in return (although Ofsted did say it might review this aspect of its rules). The situation arose when a police officer was warned by Ofsted to end a reciprocal arrangement with her colleague, another officer. She told the *Mail on Sunday* (27 September 2009): 'When the Ofsted inspector turned up, the first thing she said was: "I have had a report that you're running an illegal childminding business"'.

The Ofsted Childcare Register applies only to childcarers living in England. The Childcare Approval Scheme in Wales is run by Nestor and was launched in 2007, and enables parents in Wales who use an approved childcarer to apply for tax credits. Both schemes are voluntary for child carers who are not required to register, such as nannies and over-eights childminders. They have a childcare qualification or have taken an introductory course, hold a valid first-aid certificate and have had an enhanced CRB disclosure. The childcare element of the Working Tax Credit is also available to parents using registered or approved childcare.

Checklist

Advantages of a childminder:

- registered with and regularly inspected by Ofsted (or Childcare Approval Scheme in Wales) for under-eightss;
- more one-to-one than nurseries;
- self-employed;
- siblings can be looked after together;
- your child will mix with children of different ages;
- they care for small groups of children;
- they have a medical check, their own public liability insurance and a valid first-aid certificate (if registered); and
- some childminders are 'accredited' and able to deliver early years education as part of the free nursery education entitlement (see below).

Advantages of a nanny:

- can be approved under the government's Childcare Approval Scheme or the Ofsted Childcare Register in England;
- one-to-one care in your own home;
- siblings can be looked after together;
- parents retain control of the child's routine, diet, etc.; and
- greater flexibility of hours.

What's a 'CRB check'?

A CRB (as in Criminal Records Bureau) check is a document containing information held by the police and government departments which can be used by employers and voluntary organisations to make safer recruitment decisions. Disclosures are provided by the Criminal Records Bureau, part of the Home Office. It is necessary for those regularly caring for, training, supervising or being in sole charge of children and contains details of convictions including spent convictions, plus details of any cautions, reprimands or warnings. It also involves an extra level of checking with local police force records in addition to checks with the Police National Computer (PNC) and the government department lists of those who are legally barred from work with children.

How do you find a childminder?

Your local children's information service can give you a list of registered childminders. You can find details of your nearest at the ChildcareLink website. You could also try your local children's centre, which should keep a list of childminding vacancies in the area. If you're looking for an over-eights childminder, you could try your local school to see if they keep a list. It is recommended that you see a number of childminders, at least two or three, ideally when the children are there and you can see whether the atmosphere is happy and busy. It is a good idea to ask the childminder to show you around their house, including the bathroom, and the places where your child will sleep, eat and play. Another tip is to take your child with you and see whether they are welcomed into the group. If the childminder is a member of a professional scheme, such as the National Childminding Association's Quality First scheme, it is another sign of commitment towards their continuing professional development. They will agree to work towards quality standards which cover safety, nutrition, managing children's behaviour as well as business practice. Registered childminders can develop their careers through the Council for Awards in Children's Care and Education (CACHE) diploma in home-based childcare, or the Early Years Professional Status.

How do you find a nanny?

You could advertise in the local paper or in a specialist magazine or contact local colleges which offer childcare courses. There are also nanny agencies, which charge a fee to find you a list of suitable nannies. A good agency will carry out its own checks on nannies listed with them.

Useful tips on interviewing nannies include:

- asking a friend, a partner or relative to sit in on the interview to provide a second opinion;

- inviting prospective candidates back for a second 'working interview';

- introducing the children to the candidate at the second interview to see if they establish a rapport; agreeing a trial period before the nanny accepts the job full time, anywhere between one week and three months; and

- trusting your own instincts so that even if the person has the best qualifications and highest recommendations, if the appointment does not feel right, keep looking.

You are thinking of employing a nanny. What do you need to know?

First things first, you will be an employer with the same legal responsibilities as any other kind of employer. This means you have to meet certain obligations, including paying tax and National Insurance Contributions as well as ensuring minimum standards of employment. If you employ a nanny in the UK and you pay them more than £125 per week (in the 2009/10 tax year), you have the same legal responsibilities as a commercial employer and the law requires you to:

- register as an employer;

- run a PAYE (Pay As You Earn) scheme;

- keep tax records on their behalf;

- provide regular payslips;

- provide them with an employment contract;

- pay regular Income Tax and National Insurance Contributions;

- pay employer's National Insurance Contributions; and

- file an employer's annual tax return.

These obligations also apply if your nanny earns (at the time of going to press) less than £95 per week in your employment but more than £110 in total (if, for example, they have two part-time jobs); is in short-term employment; and works in the UK (irrespective of the country of origin of the nanny or employer).

Nannies are often paid cash in hand. The arrangement is not good for them (no National Insurance Contributions), arguably not ideal for your children if it is a less than formal relationship and certainly no good for HM Revenue & Customs. Failure to register as an employer if you are paying your nanny above the weekly threshold is a criminal offence, which can lead to heavy penalties and unwelcome publicity. There are companies such as Nannytax which provide payroll services taking on the employer responsibilities.

Employing a nanny – checklist

P45: Whenever your nanny leaves your employment you are required by law to provide them with a P45 (summarising pay and tax received in your employment and allows the next employee to deduct the correct amount of Income Tax).

Tax and other payments: Most nanny employers are classed as small employers and are only required to pay tax and National Insurance once a quarter.

Redundancy pay: If you no longer have a job for your nanny and they have been employed by you for two years or more, then they are entitled to redundancy pay, just like any other employee. If your circumstances change and you no longer have a full-time job for your nanny (e.g. perhaps your children go to school full time) and you want to employ a nanny on a part-time basis, you are required to first offer the 'new' position to the existing nanny. If they choose not to continue working under the new conditions, you are still required to pay them redundancy pay, unless they are on a fixed-term contract.

Statutory holiday pay: All employees in the UK are entitled by law to 28 days' paid leave every year. This includes all bank holidays. This entitlement now begins from the first day of employment but cannot be taken until it has been accrued. Part-time employees are entitled to the pro-rata equivalent. Employers whose nannies do not accompany them on holidays may like to agree with their nannies, when employment starts, that at least part of this entitlement is to be taken when they themselves are on holiday.

Statutory maternity pay: If your nanny becomes pregnant and is in your employment at a specific qualifying date, then you, as employer, are required by law to pay statutory maternity pay, even if she subsequently leaves your employment before her period of maternity leave commences. You might be able to reclaim this from the Contributions Agency.

Statutory sick pay: If your nanny is unable to work through sickness, then they are entitled to statutory sick pay after the first three (working) days of absence. The first three days of absence are considered waiting days and the nanny or other employee is not legally entitled to SSP. Some parents give their nannies incentives (e.g. an afternoon off or HMV vouchers) if they don't take time off sick over a certain period.

National Minimum Wage: It is a criminal offence for an employer to pay below the National Minimum Wage, with a fine on conviction (see chapter 7. Nannies who live as part of the family household and are not provided with separate accommodation are excluded.

Working time regulations: The European Working Time Directive grants all employees a minimum 28 days paid holiday per year and rest breaks (however, nannies and all other domestic employees are exempt from the measures concerning working hours).

Insurance: You need to make sure that your household insurance policy includes employer's liability insurance to protect you if your nanny has an accident during working hours. Employer's liability insurance is often included as standard in most policies, but check your policy documents with your home insurance provider. Employers face steep fines if insurance is not in place.

Student loans: If your nanny has a student loan that they took out after August 1998 and if their salary exceeds £15,000 per annum they are required to make regular repayments starting after they leave their course. You should pay these contributions directly.

Taxable benefits: If you provide your nanny with a car for their private use, or any other benefits in kind, both you and they may be liable to pay some additional tax and National Insurance Contributions on these items. If you have agreed a fixed net wage with them then you should be aware that any additional liability would fall entirely on you.

Do you need to have an employment contract for your nanny?

All parents acting as employers must provide their nannies with an employment contract or statement of terms and conditions of their employment within two months of the start date. Review your contract regularly and make sure that any changes agreed are written down, signed by both parties and dated.

You need to discuss the job with your nanny and make time to go through and agree the contract. It should clearly set out all aspects of the job and forms a legally binding agreement between you and your nanny. It is recommended that it should cover:

- the job description and hours of work;
- salary and agreed method of payment;
- holiday and leave allowances;
- what happens if the nanny or child is unwell;
- payment of expenses;
- house rules (and details of accommodation, if live-in);
- behaviour management agreement;
- permission for outings, bathing children, applying sunblock, taking photographs, etc.; and
- notice period.

What should you include in a childminder agreement?

By law, self-employed childminders must have a written agreement with you. You can use a model agreement (e.g. the National Childminding Association contract). Some things that you need to agree on are:

- how much the childminder charges;

- extra costs; for example, to provide for meals, toiletries or outings;

- times that the childminder is available;

- extra fees; for example, on public holidays or out of working hours;

- family holiday arrangements;

- what happens when you, your child or childminder is sick;

- deposits or retainer fees; and

- notice period.

It is a good idea to have a separate contract for each child you place with the childminder, and to review your contract with your childminder every six or 12 months. If you (or the childminder) want to end the contract or change arrangements, then you should give the other notice in writing. If you are unable or unwilling to wait for the notice period to end, you must pay the childcare fees that would have been due during that notice period.

How do you go about choosing a nursery?

The National Day Nurseries Association (NDNA) suggests a number of steps:

1. Ensure that the nursery you choose is registered with Ofsted (the registration certificate should be displayed together with a current certificate of insurance).

2. Check to see if it belongs to a professional organisation (such as the NDNA).

3. Ask to see recent Ofsted reports.

4. Ask if the nursery has gained any Kitemarks of excellence.

You should satisfy yourself on the following points:

- Is there a safe and clean outside play area?

- Is the interior bright, warm, clean, well decorated and welcoming?

- Is the equipment of good quality, clean, safe and appropriate?

- What sort of meals are provided (can they provide for special diets and are menus changed on a regular basis)?

- Do the staff and children look happy? Check staff-to-child ratios (as a guide, it should be about 1:3 for 0–2 years; 1:4 for 2–3 years; and 1:8 for 3–8 years).

- The NDNA reckons half of the staff must hold relevant childcare qualifications such as NVQ Childcare level 2 or equivalent. One member of staff should have a first-aid certificate and all supervisors are required to have an NVQ Childcare level 3 or equivalent.

Are you entitled to a free nursery place for your child?

All children are entitled to up to two years of free early education before reaching statutory school age (in other words, the first term following their fifth birthday). At the time of going to press, the minimum free entitlement for three- and four-year-olds is 12.5 hours a week for 38 weeks a year. This nursery education may be delivered in a nursery or with an accredited childminder. The right to or guarantee of a free part-time early education place is a right to a free place in your local area, not the right to a free place with a particular provider.

Can you change your working hours to spend more time looking after your child?

Mothers often want to work part time or make other changes to their working hours after maternity leave – for example, avoiding evening shifts so as to be at home for children's mealtimes and bedtimes. Many are told by their employers that there is no right to go part time, but there is more to it than this.

Any parent of a child under the age of six (or, if your child is disabled and receives a disability living allowance, under the age of 18) has a right to make a 'flexible working request' to their employer, once they have been employed for 26 weeks. This can be a request for any change to the hours you work, the times at which you are expected to be at work, or the place from which you work. So you could request to work three days a week in the office and one day a week from home, or that you still work the same number of hours but start earlier and finish earlier than other staff. The employer must arrange a meeting with you to discuss your request, and must then inform you of the decision and the reasons for it. If your request is refused, you have the right to an appeal, to a higher manager if possible. However, your rights are purely 'procedural'; you cannot ask a tribunal to overturn your employer's decision – at least, not under the flexible working legislation. The government's hope is that by requiring employers to seriously consider an employee's request, many will be granted.

However, your rights are actually greater if you are a woman and the reason for your request is to enable you to better look after your children. Because women still bear the brunt of childcare responsibility in society, any working arrangements that are not 'family-friendly' may be viewed by an employment tribunal as a form of 'indirect sex discrimination' if the employer cannot objectively justify those arrangements by showing that they meet a business objective and are reasonably necessary. You could bring your case to a tribunal and ask it to consider whether your employer should have let you change your hours. It will consider whether your job could be done on a part-time or job-share basis, the extent to which part of your responsibilities could be shifted to other workers, and the overall cost to the employer, balanced against the disadvantage you are likely to suffer if your request is not granted.

CONTACTS

To find out more about childminding, see the National Childminding Association webiste (www.ncma.org.uk) and for information on its Children Come First childminding networks, see www.ncmaccf.org.uk. For details about childcare and registration requirements, see www.ofsted.gov.uk (Ofsted publishes an updated information sheet for parents explaining the differences between childcarers who must register and those who can opt to register, Information for Parents and Carers Using Childcare Services) and www.childcareapprovalschemewales.co.uk. For information about local services, see www.childcarelink.gov.uk.

To find out more about employing a nanny, read *Employing an Approved Childcarer*, see www.childcareapprovalscheme.co.uk; plus there is guidance about choosing a nursery at the National Day Nurseries Association website (www.ndna.org.uk).

CHAPTER 4

Education: early years

School life is such a significant and formative part of your child's life and we have divided our coverage of it across two chapters. The first considers the kind of schooling that your children might receive. Increasingly, a parent's relationship with the education system is prescribed by rules and regulations. As is discussed later in this chapter, there are over 50,000 appeals a year made by disappointed parents unhappy with the schools allocated to their children. 'Soaring numbers of parents' were launching appeals against the state schools allocated to their children 'amid a growing shortage of places', reported the *Daily Mail* (30 October 2009). Competition was 'so intense' that many were instructing lawyers 'at a cost of up to £2,000 to help them fight decisions to send their children to their second, third or even sixth choice schools'.

This chapter starts by looking at your child's entitlement to a free education and your responsibility for the education of your child (e.g. whether you can teach your child in your own home). We then look at your choice of school and, increasingly pertinently, what a parent can do if they are refused their choice of school. Finally, we provide an overview of the different kinds of schools that are available.

Do your children have the right to a free education?

The Education Act 1944 gave us the legislative framework for modern schooling. This landmark Act introduced free schooling for all children aged 5 to 14 years. The age limit was lifted to 15 years in 1947 and then to

16 years in 1972. By law, compulsory education for all children begins in the term following their fifth birthday and ends on the last Friday in June in the school year in which the child reaches 16 years. Your child can't leave school until that date. From 2013 over-16-year-olds will have to take part in education or work-based training. In other words, young people will still be able to leave school at 16 and get a job but it must involve some education and/or training.

Who is responsible for the education of your child?

You are. There is a legal responsibility on parents to ensure that a child of 'school age' receives full-time education according to age, ability or aptitude under the Education Act 1996. Parents are committing an offence if they fail to do so. Prosecution could result in a fine of up to £2,500 or even a jail sentence of up to three months. Alternatively, education welfare officers, police officers and head teachers can issue penalty notices to parents of between £50 and £100 and failure to pay can lead to prosecution. Local authorities are responsible under the law for making sure parents fulfil their responsibility of ensuring that their child receives an education.

Is it breaking the law not to send your kids to school?

Education is compulsory up to the age of 16, but school isn't. Home education is a long-established legal right in the UK. It has been estimated that as many as 170,000 children are educated at home in England and Wales. Many parents consider home education because they encounter a particular problem, such as bullying, or have concerns about the quality of the teaching or special needs provision. Increasingly, home education is being considered as an option if a family fails to secure a place for its child at the school of their choice. Others might object to schooling for philosophical, political or religious reasons.

The legal responsibility for parents under the 1996 Education Act is only that their children are provided a suitable education 'at school or otherwise'. You do not have to have any formal qualifications in order to be able to educate your child at home. Sometimes parents are under the impression that their rights are taken away if their child has a statement of special needs – see chapter 5. This is not true. Many families choose to home educate children with special needs. You need permission from your local authority to remove your child from a special school. At the time of going to press the government is consulting on changes to the home education system, including possible registration and monitoring proposals (see below). In January 2009 the government launched new guidance on children missing education and announced a review of home education focusing on the concern that the current system did not give local authorities adequate powers to 'support and monitor the education, safety and wellbeing of home-educated children'.

If you home-school ...

... do you have to operate like a 'real' school?

No, you can work on what you want and when you want to. You do not need a timetable nor do you have to follow the National Curriculum although you can if you want. Home-education enthusiasts note that you have the freedom to arrange your learning around the individual requirements of your child and the family, without restricting yourself to 'school hours' and term times.

... will your local authority monitor what you are doing?

Your local authority has a duty to make sure that you are providing a proper education for your child. Currently it doesn't have an automatic right of access to your home but the review of home education has recommended that the local authority should have the right to access your home and be able to speak to your child out of your presence. The review also recommends that parents provide local authorities with a plan for the child's education. In the meantime it is likely that it will want to know what educational provision is being made for your child.

... what about exams?

Formal testing is not required – your child does not have to sit Key Stage tests (Standard Attainment Tests (SATs) only apply to state schools). If you do want to take exams – and you are not legally obliged to do so – then it's possible to work for them at home. You may have to go to an examination centre to sit papers, and you will also have to pay the costs involved, but you do have the advantage of selecting the board whose external syllabus most suits your child. One possible advantage for home-educated children is that they are free to sit exams when they are ready for them. Technical colleges, further education colleges and night schools can offer flexible courses of study for GCSEs or other qualifications to young people under and over the age of 16. Others use correspondence courses. Again, you and your child must decide what is right for them.

... won't my child miss out socially?

Obviously that will depend upon the environment that you provide for your children. The support group Education Otherwise insists that home education does not have to be socially isolated. It says: 'In a natural community children spend their daily lives with old people, babies, and everyone in between. They do not compete, but learn to search out the needs of others and to help them live and learn. This mixed age group and habit of teaching and helping others, and being helped and taught by people younger or older than oneself, is a natural part of home education.'

... what notice do you need to give?

If your child has never been to school, there is currently no action for you to take prior to starting home education. However, following its review of home education, the government is proposing to introduce arrangements for the registration of all home-educated children. Campaigners opposing the proposal say it amounts to 'licensing' home educators and feel that parents, not the local authority, should decide what represents a suitable education. Currently if you are withdrawing a child from school then you must formally de-register by writing to the head teacher. The school then informs the local authority.

Do you have the right to choose your child's school?

No; you don't have a right to choose a school, but you do have a right to express your choice of state school. There are rights that parents can expect from the school admissions process, chiefly:

- your child has the right to a place in school between the ages of five and 16 years;

- you have the right to say which school you would prefer your child to go to – although the right to state a preference does not guarantee your child a place at that school;

- your local authority must offer your child a school place; and

- you have a right to appeal if your child is not offered a place at their preferred school – see later.

What expectations can you have from the school admissions process?

To a degree, every child aged between five and 16 years old is entitled by law to a place at a state school, but this is not an automatic process – you must apply. Admission to the state school of your choice (primary or secondary) isn't automatic. All schools have a list of 'admissions criteria'.

Before you send in your application, or apply online, it is useful to know what that process is; in particular, the criteria you need to take into consideration before applying and the key deadline dates for primary and secondary applications.

Local authorities must allow parents to express their preference as to which school their child is to be educated under the School Standards and Framework Act 1998. Usually there are only limited grounds on which the admissions authority (local authorities for community schools and governing bodies for voluntary-aided, foundation and trust schools and academies, see below) can refuse admission.

How can you appeal a decision to refuse your child your first-choice school?

Every year, some 1.5 million children start schools and in 2006/07 there were 56,610 appeals made by disappointed parents in England unhappy with the schools allocated to their children. More than one-third of appeals heard were decided in their parents' favour (34.4 per cent).

In most cases the reason for refusing a place is that admission will cause 'prejudice' to the efficient use of resources or efficient education – in other words, this means that an additional admission will over-stretch the school.

For Key Stage 1 applications, which include reception and academic years 1 and 2 (see chapter 5 for a guide to Key Stages), you can also be turned down if the class has reached the legal limit of 30 pupils per qualified teacher. See class size appeals below. At secondary level your child can be turned down for failing to reach the required standard for a grammar school.

The Department for Children, Schools and Families has produced codes of practice on school admissions and school admissions appeals (these can be downloaded from its website) providing guidance on how admissions and appeals should be conducted. You will find out if you have been successful between March and May for a primary school place; for secondary schools an offer must be posted to you by 1 March. If your application is unsuccessful, you will be entitled to a statutory appeal that will be heard by an independent appeal panel.

There are different kinds of appeals:

- **Normal 'prejudice' appeals:** These are all appeals except those relating to grammar schools and class sizes. In these appeals, the published admissions criteria or the school's published admissions number (i.e. the number of pupils the school must admit before refusing you a place) does not bind the panel. It will consider each appeal on its own merits.

  The panel will apply three tests to the evidence presented. First, it will consider the published admissions arrangements and will have to decide if they have been applied correctly in your case and that a mistake was not made in refusing to admit your child. Secondly, the panel will have to consider whether any more admissions will cause 'prejudice' (or damage the ability of the school to provide education) at the school. The obligation is on the admissions authority to demonstrate why any more admissions will cause problems for the school. It is not up to you to show that an admission will not cause problems. In practice, many parents will try to show that an admission will not cause any such problems. Finally, the panel will consider the personal reasons why you want your child to attend the school and it will have to consider if these reasons are sufficiently compelling to outweigh any prejudice to the school.

The panel operates as a quasi-judicial body and written evidence supported by an independent third party carries a lot of weight. This is usually the case if you are claiming medical reasons and you have the written support of your GP or a consultant.

The grounds for an appeal are usually the reasons why you picked the school in the first place. There are many reasons why parents pick particular schools but these usually come under certain categories (e.g. medical, educational, social, community, environmental, etc.).

Although the appeal is principally concerned with the preferred school, it is quite legitimate to express concerns about the allocated school. However, you have to be very careful how this is done. Usually these concerns will be to do with the educational record of the school or the logistical difficulties in getting to and from the school.

The local authority where you live has a legal responsibility to find a school place for your child but this is usually done by allocating a place at a school that is nearest to you which has places available. This will be done after all other places have been allocated. Therefore the schools with places still available will be where parents, for whatever reason, have chosen not to send their children. Again, there will be a range of reasons but it may be because the school is not perceived to be a good school or it has a bad reputation.

- **Grammar school appeals:** If your child has failed the 11-plus (the exam faced by some students in the last year of their primary education), you can lodge an appeal. However, at these appeals, the appeal panel will have to decide if your child is suitable for a grammar school place. You can put forward mitigating circumstances as to why your child did not perform better. It may be that they were not feeling well on the day of the test or there were family problems that put them off. However, you will need to provide written evidence to support these claims; for example, if your child was feeling unwell you will need to provide evidence from your doctor.

In order to convince the panel that your child is suitable for a grammar school you will need to obtain the written support from their existing head teacher and also to supply a copy of their most recent school report with predicted SATs scores.

- **Class size appeals:** For reception or academic years 1 and 2, the statutory class size is 30 where there is only one qualified teacher present. If you are refused a place because the class has reached its 30 limit, the grounds of appeal are limited. You can argue either that the admissions authority made a mistake in dealing with the application that denied a place, or that the decision taken by the admissions authority was unreasonable based on the information that it had received when a decision was reached. These appeals are difficult to win (the success rate in England is about 18 per cent).

  You can submit whatever information and evidence you want but the panel will only be able to take it into account if it comes within the two grounds referred to above.

  In some cases the class may have fewer than 30 pupils but still be full. In these cases this will not be a class size appeal and your appeal will be heard on the basis of normal 'prejudice' explained above.

  For smaller schools, however, the school may be able to claim class size prejudice even if this will not occur until years 1 or 2. For example, if the intake is 45 with two teachers in reception it may seem possible to take extra pupils without breaching class size limits. But if the school then combines different age groups in years 1 and 2 to form three classes of 30 pupils each with only one teacher per class, an extra pupil would mean one class was over the limit. If the panel decides that it is not a class size appeal, then the appeal will revert to a normal prejudice appeal described above.

You're moving to the country with your five-year-old but the local infant school is full. What do you do?

The infant class size legislation means that the school must not normally take more than 30 pupils. However, when a child moves into an area outside the normal admissions round, and there is no other school within a reasonable distance of home, the law (specifically, the Education (Infant Class Sizes) (England) Regulations 1998) allows the school to admit the child as an 'excepted pupil'. If no child leaves during the school year, the school would have to take action to reduce the pupil:teacher ratio, which could mean employing another teacher.

What are the various types of school available to your children and what are the differences between them?

A 'school' is defined in law as an educational institution that is outside the further and higher education sectors. There are several main types of school:

- **Community schools:** The local authority employs staff on behalf of the governing body, owns the school's land and buildings and is the admissions authority. The council has primary responsibility for deciding the arrangements for admitting pupils to the schools.

- **Foundation schools:** The land and buildings are owned by the governing body or by a charitable foundation. The governing body is the employer and has primary responsibility for deciding arrangements for admitting pupils to the school.

- **Trust schools:** A new type of foundation school with a trust formed by a voluntary organisation, faith group, parents' group, private firm or university. They are similar to foundation schools, employing their own staff and deciding their own arrangements for admitting pupils to the school, but the governing body may be made up of a majority of trust governors, meaning fewer parent governors.

- **Voluntary-aided schools:** Mostly faith schools where the school's land and buildings will normally be owned by a charitable foundation. The governing body will contribute towards the capital costs of running the school. It is the employer and has primary responsibility for deciding the arrangements for admitting pupils to the school.

- **Voluntary-controlled schools:** Where the local authority employs the staff on behalf of the governing body and has primary responsibility for deciding the arrangements for admitting pupils to the schools.

- **Academies and city technology colleges:** Publicly funded independent schools with financial sponsors and specialisms. Academies employ their own staff and decide arrangements for admitting pupils to the school. They provide free education but decide the curriculum and governance. Their funding agreements with the Department for Children, Schools and Families set out how they should operate, generally taking account of government guidance, but operating outside education legislation.

- **Special schools:** Provide education for children with special educational needs (although most are educated in ordinary schools) – see later. Most are maintained (i.e. state) schools; others are non-maintained (usually run by charities on a non-profit-making basis); and others are independent special schools.

- **Independent schools:** Outside the state school system, there are approximately 2,300 independent schools in England and they obtain most of their income from fees paid by parents and investment. Just over half of all independent schools have charitable status.

Most state schools are non-selective but selective secondary schools still exist in the state sector. Grammar schools which select all their pupils on academic ability operate in some areas. It is unlikely that they will increase to any great extent and even the Conservative Party has decided they are not serving the whole community. However, the party has said it would not oppose new grammar schools in areas that already have secondary selection. Some comprehensive schools select up to ten per cent of their intake on aptitude for a particular subject. Most comprehensive schools, which cater for children of all abilities, are also specialist schools or colleges focusing extra resources and lesson time on a particular subject area such as modern languages or sport.

CONTACTS

For information on home education, see www.education-otherwise.org; www.home-education.org.uk and www.he-special.org.uk. To find out about school appeals, see www.schoolappeals.org.uk and the Department for Children, Schools and Families webiste, which has codes of practice on school admissions and school admissions appeals (www.dcsf.gov.uk). There is more information on both admissions and appeals at www.ace-ed.org.uk.

CHAPTER 5

Education: school-life

This chapter continues our look at school life. It is divided into the following sections:

- **In the classroom:** We look at what children are taught in the classroom and explain how the National Curriculum provides a legal framework for the education of our children. The section also considers the content of school lessons and what powers, if any, you have if you object to aspects of your child's learning such as religious or sex education.

- **Your child's welfare:** This section begins with discipline and considers whether, for example, teachers can hold your child back in detention after school hours or carry out corporal punishment. It then looks at the exclusion regime and you and your child's rights if they are excluded.

  We also cover how children should be treated if they are bullied or called racist names.

  The next area is your responsibility for your child's attendance. What if his school disapproves of your plans for an extended holiday, or if your child fails to attend school regularly?

  Then we consider your child's right to a good diet at school – from entitlement to free school lunches, free milk and what you can do if you aren't happy with what's on their tray.

  Finally, in this section we consider health and safety issues – from concerns about the inappropriate behaviour of staff to the school's responsibility if your child is injured on a school activity.

- **Special educational needs:** This section considers how you might secure the appropriate education for your child if they have such needs.

- **Playing a part in your child's schooling:** Here we cover how parents can play a part in their child's school by becoming a school governor or parent governor representative.

- **Problems with your school:** The final section deals with problems at school and how best to deal with them, including what is the best way to handle a complaint and, finally, whether it is possible to take legal action against a school.

In the classroom

What is the National Curriculum, and how does it work?

The government did not prescribe the nature of what was taught in schools in England and Wales and how pupils were taught until the 1980s. Although there was a legal framework for Religious Education (RE), generally it was up to local authorities and teachers to come up with the curriculum. It was the Conservative government under Margaret Thatcher that removed powers from local education authorities following concerns about apparent political bias and the endorsement of homosexuality by local education authorities. The government eventually introduced the National Curriculum under the Education Reform Act 1988. Since then the National Curriculum has undergone a number of changes including a radical slimming down in size and the introduction of greater flexibility in what must be taught to pupils in their last two years of compulsory education.

The National Curriculum provides a blueprint which attempts to make sure that teaching standards are universally consistent. It sets out 'the most important knowledge and skills that every child has a right to learn'; imposes 'a flexible framework given to teachers by government, so that all school children are taught in a way that is balanced and manageable but stretching enough to challenge them and meet their diverse needs'; and gives 'standards that measure how well children are doing ... so teachers can monitor achievement'.

It also defines your child's progress in 'Key Stages'. At the end of Key Stage 2 your child will take national tests called 'SATs'. National tests are no longer taken at the end of Key Stages 1 and 3 although optional tests are available for the school to check whether your child is making progress at any point it feels appropriate. You should be informed of how they have performed in such tests but the results will not be published as a league table alongside those of other pupils and schools. At the end of Key Stage 4, they will sit national examinations, such as GCSEs (see box).

The SATs are as much to measure the effectiveness of the school as the progress your child is making. If inspectors feel that not enough pupils are making good progress, they can take measures which can result in the school having to take action to put things right. Ultimately the school can be closed if it does not improve quickly enough. Ofsted inspectors will also check that the school is teaching what it is meant to teach and will report on any shortcomings.

Key Stages			
Age	**Stage**	**Year**	**Tests**
3 to 4	Foundation		
4 to 5	Foundation		
5 to 6	Key Stage 1	Year 1	
6 to 7	Key Stage 1	Year 2	
7 to 8	Key Stage 2	Year 3	
8 to 9	Key Stage 2	Year 4	
9 to 10	Key Stage 2	Year 5	
10 to 11	Key Stage 2	Year 6	National tests
11 to 12	Key Stage 3	Year 7	
12 to 13	Key Stage 3	Year 8	
13 to 14	Key Stage 3	Year 9	
14 to 15	Key Stage 4	Year 10	Some children take GCSEs early
15 to 16	Key Stage 4	Year 11	Most children take GCSEs or other national qualifications

What if you object to what your child is taught?

Despite the National Curriculum setting out what schools must teach, there is still scope for controversy although what is controversial changes with the times. In the past, political indoctrination and sex education were issues of great concern. The Little Red Schoolbook passed round the classrooms of the 1970s told children more about the birds and the bees than many adults could accept. Today the major concern is whether faith schools divide communities and how far religious teaching should go. Clearly schools in the UK are there to promote debate and a free exchange of ideas but in the case of some controversial topics, the law (to some extent) prescribes what should or should not be covered in lessons – see box.

Politics, religion and sex – what your child can and can't be taught:

- **Too political?** Schools are expressly required by statute to forbid 'the pursuit of partisan political activities' for pupils under 12 years and 'the promotion of partisan political views in the teaching of any subject in the school' (Education Act 1996).

- **Gay rights?** There was a furore over section 28 (of the Local Government Act 1988) after it was amended during the Thatcher era to prohibit the 'promotion of homosexuality' by local authorities and the teaching in state schools of 'pretended family relationships' (i.e. lesbian and gay). That controversial legislation was scrapped in 2003. Government guidance says that schools deal with issues to do with sexual orientation sensitively and honestly. A survey in 2003 of 300 secondary schools in England and Wales found 82 per cent of teachers aware of verbal incidents of homophobia and 26 per cent aware of physical incidents. Government guidance on bullying says schools should challenge homophobic language and include homophobic bullying in their anti-bullying policies.

- **Religion?** Community, foundation, trust and voluntary schools have a duty to ensure that all pupils take part in a daily 'act of collective worship' (School Standards and Framework Act 1998). In schools without a particular religious identity, this must be of 'broadly Christian character' reflecting 'the broad traditions of

Christian belief without being distinctive of any particular Christian denomination'. In a foundation, trust or voluntary school with a religious identity, then worship will be in keeping with any trust deed or the particular denomination. Parents have the unqualified right to withdraw their children from collective worship or Religious Education again under the 1998 Act. A head teacher might apply to their local standing advisory council on Religious Education if they want to change the degree to which there is a Christian element to the worship reflecting, perhaps, the community the school's pupils belong to.

Local authorities and schools must ensure that Religious Education (RE) is provided (again, the School Standards and Framework Act 1998). In schools without a strong religious identity, the syllabus might be wide and there are restrictions in law preventing too narrow a focus on a particular denomination. In foundation and voluntary-controlled schools with a religious character, governors must provide RE for not more than two periods a week. In voluntary-aided schools of a religious character, RE will reflect the particular religious denomination. RE is not part of the National Curriculum.

- **Sex?** The law does, to a limited extent, prescribe how difficult issues, such as sex, are tackled at school. If you have particular concerns, then it is a good idea to raise these first of all with the class teacher, head of year or head teacher.

All pupils in secondary education must be offered sex and relationship education. While some aspects such as reproduction are taught as part of the National Curriculum, much is taught through the non-statutory elements of Personal, Social and Health Education (PSHE). From 2010 primary schools too will have to teach children about personal relationships and the biological aspects of sex. Governing bodies of maintained schools must have their own policies for providing sex education and together with heads must ensure that when sex education is given children 'learn the nature of marriage and its importance for family life and the bringing up of children, and they are protected from teaching and materials which are inappropriate', taking into account their age, and religious and cultural background (Education Act 1996, section 403). Sex education includes education about HIV, AIDS and other sexually transmitted diseases.

Can schools teach your children about creationism?

Yes, but as a belief not as an alternative to scientific explanations. Religious education is currently the most contentious area of the curriculum with accusations that academies, in particular, are giving undue prominence to the teaching of creationism or intelligent design – a literal belief that the world was created in six days and that life is too complex to be accounted for by evolution.

Creationism is not a stand-alone National Curriculum subject area but could be studied alongside a range of religions and other beliefs. The Qualifications and Curriculum Authority (the quango that oversees the National Curriculum) has recently developed a unit for pupils to study the relationship between religion (including creationism) and science.

Academies are not subject to the National Curriculum requirements although most will use it as a model. Those academies sponsored by Christian millionaire Sir Peter Vardey have been particularly criticised for pushing religious beliefs such as creationism (although this is denied by their sponsor). The academies within his Emmanuel Foundation do, however, have a strongly religious ethos.

The debate has taken place in the context of concern about racial and religious divisions in society and their role in fermenting the racial disturbances in northern towns and cities in 2001. A government review has warned that schools needed to do more to overcome those divisions.

Do you have any rights over what your child is taught about sex?

Parents have the right to stop their child taking part in all or part of any sex education that is not part of the National Curriculum (under the Education Act 1996). If for whatever reason there are concerns, you should write to the school's governing body requesting a copy of the school's sex education and relationships policy, which must include information about how parents can withdraw their child from sex education. This right does not extend to withdrawal from lessons on reproduction, which form part of the science curriculum.

The law on confidential advice to children dates back to 1985 when

Victoria Gillick lost her fight to stop doctors prescribing the contraceptive pill to girls under 16 without their parents' knowledge. The court ruled that it was lawful for doctors to put under-16s on the pill if the children were regarded as intelligent enough to understand what was involved. That judgment introduced what are known as the 'Fraser guidelines' by which it could be determined whether a child was 'Gillick' competent – see chapter 6. In other words, whether she could understand the advice; that she couldn't be persuaded to tell her parents; and that her physical or mental health would suffer without contraception.

Your child's welfare

How should you prepare for a parents' evening?

This is the opportunity to raise concerns directly with your child's teacher if you have issues to do with your child's welfare. A school will invite you to attend parents' evenings at least once a year where you can find out how your child is doing and meet your child's teachers. The Department for Children, Schools and Families recommends that parents prepare beforehand. In particular, it recommends:

- if you receive a report before the evening, spend time with your child going through it. Look at all areas and not just academic achievement, but also behaviour and attendance;

- if you do not receive a report, still spend some time with your child talking about strengths and weaknesses, perhaps looking at grades, marks and comments on homework and coursework; and

- make a note of any questions you want to ask the teachers; include concerns about emotional and social progress.

It is a good idea to check whether you should take your child with you or not.

A new approach?

Children's well-being is of increasing concern to schools. A UNICEF report in 2007 ranked the UK in the bottom third of economically advanced nations for 'child well-being'. The government consulted children about what they wanted from their childhood and came up with the five goals which form the basis of the Every Child Matters initiative (which was the result of a 2003 report into the death of Victoria Climbié, the eight-year-old girl who was abused and murdered by her guardians). The goals are:

- be healthy;

- stay safe;

- enjoy and achieve;

- make a positive contribution; and

- achieve economic well-being.

Schools and local authorities are inspected on how they are achieving the goals and government policy increasingly emphasises not only educational achievement, but also the wider well-being of the child both in and out of school.

What authority does a school have to discipline your child?

There is now an explicit power to discipline pupils (the Education and Inspections Act 2006). Until then a school's power to do so was based on the common law concept of being *in loco parentis* (meaning 'acting in place of a parent').

Each school must have its own discipline policy based on principles agreed by its governors. It should include a code of conduct for pupils. Conduct rules can apply before and after school as well as during the school day and schools can discipline their pupils for behaviour off school premises where this has an impact on the school; for example, shoplifting in school uniform. The kinds of sanctions a school might use include reprimands; a letter to parents or carers; removal from a class or group; loss of privileges such as use of computers at break time; detention or exclusion.

If you disagree with the way your school is treating your child, raise the issue first with the teachers and then the head teacher. If that doesn't resolve the matter, you can complain to the governing body. For more details on school complaints, see the 'Problems with your school' section.

Does a school have the right to keep your child back after school?

Yes; schools have the right to use detentions if pupils behave badly. They must give parents at least 24 hours' notice (except where the detention is at lunchtime) before keeping your child in detention so you can make alternative arrangements for transport or childcare. Schools recently acquired greater powers and flexibility to use detentions under the Education and Inspections Act 2006. In particular, it allows detentions to be held at weekends and on staff training days without parental consent.

Are teachers allowed to hit or cane your child?

Corporal punishment (e.g. caning and smacking) has been outlawed in schools in England and Wales since the late 1980s and legislation (the Education (no. 2) Act 1986) removed the legal immunity for teachers from charges of battery.

While corporal punishment is illegal, teachers are allowed by law to use what is called 'reasonable force' to prevent a child from committing an offence, injuring others or himself, or causing disruption. So leading a child by the arm might be used, for example, to enforce an instruction to leave a classroom. What is 'reasonable' depends on circumstances such as the age and size of the child, any disability or special educational needs they may have, the reasons for the force and the risks involved. Parents who feel that teachers have behaved unreasonably in using force should make a complaint to the governing body of the school. If the force amounts to an assault, you should make an immediate complaint to the head teacher and, in very serious cases, contact the police and social services.

What can you do if your child cannot attend a detention?

You may explain the reasons to your child's teacher or head teacher but the school may impose a fixed period exclusion if you refuse to allow your child to attend a detention. Other staff as well as teachers may impose detentions if the head teacher gives them authority.

What powers does a school have to 'exclude' your child?

Head teachers may exclude or prevent a child from attending school for a fixed period. Only the head (or a deputy, in their absence) may exclude and only for disciplinary reasons (the Education Act 2002).

Fixed period exclusions must not total more than 45 school days in any school year. Permanent exclusions should be used only as a last resort. They are generally made where a child has a track record of getting into trouble and after all other options have been tried, but a head may exclude your child for a serious one-off incident (e.g. selling drugs in school, taking a weapon into school, violence or threatened violence against another pupil or teacher, or sexual misconduct).

What rights do you have if your child is excluded?

If the school excludes your child, you have the right to write to the school's governing body telling it why you think your child shouldn't have been excluded. For some exclusions you also have the right to attend a governors' hearing to put your case. The hearing is usually held by a discipline committee of three people set up by the governing body. You must be offered a meeting if the head teacher permanently excludes your child or excludes them for fixed periods adding up to more than five school days or more in a term, or if the exclusion means they would miss a public exam.

If the head teacher excludes your child permanently and the governors uphold the exclusion, you can appeal to an independent appeal panel set up by the local authority. The governors and independent appeal panel must decide 'on the balance of probabilities' whether your child did what they are accused of. This is less than the criminal standard of proof (beyond reasonable doubt) but the more serious the accusation, the stronger the evidence should be.

You are entitled to a fair hearing and you may be able to take the independent appeal panel or the governing body to court if a governors' hearing or independent appeal hearing was not fair. You would need expert legal advice to do this. There are tight time limits for taking such action. Complaints about the running of the independent appeal panel can also go to the Local Government Ombudsman.

If your child has been excluded because of serious misbehaviour, the local authority can apply to the courts for a parenting order (see below).

If your child is excluded for more than five days, or permanently, they must be provided with alternative education from the sixth day of the exclusion. This is often in a short-stay school called a pupil referral unit.

What should a school do to protect your child from bullying?

Bullying covers a lot of ground, from name-calling, threats, violence and damage to property to socially isolating individuals, spreading nasty rumours as well as bullying by text message or email. By law a school has to have a behaviour policy, which must include measures to prevent all forms of bullying. Many schools have a separate anti-bullying policy. As a parent you have a right to a copy of any school policies.

If the bullying seems prolonged or serious, then you must speak to your child's teachers about it. Children are often, rightly, concerned that the bullying will get worse if they complain so you may need to discuss strategies with teachers on how to deal with it. Sometimes a change of seat in class or a more watchful eye at playtime can be enough. If the bullying escalates then the school will need to use the sanctions set out in its behaviour policy. If your complaints are not taken seriously, then you may have to make a formal complaint to the governing body of the school. Schools risk claims of negligence if children suffer damage as a result of bullying which the school should have prevented (see negligence below).

Your child is being called racist names at school. What should you do about it?

Schools should make sure that racial incidents are monitored. They also have a legal duty under the Race Relations (Amendment) Act 2000 to promote racial equality. Ask for a copy of your school's behaviour policy, which must make clear that racial harassment will not be tolerated and say how staff and pupils should deal with it. Make sure this happens by complaining to the head teacher in writing, giving as much detail as possible about the incidents.

What is your responsibility for ensuring your child turns up to school?

If your child is registered at a school, then you have a legal responsibility to make sure they attend school regularly and on time. Only the school can authorise your child's absence. The law provides for authorisation for the following reasons:

- illness;
- medical and dental appointments;
- days for religious observance;
- interviews;
- study leave;
- approved educational activity (e.g. school trip, off-site tuition);
- registration with a pupil referral unit or a special school (see later for further details);
- family bereavement or compassionate leave for another reason;
- any other unavoidable cause.

Schools also have discretion to authorise absence for other reasons such as family occasions or holidays.

As discussed in chapter 4, parents have a legal right to educate their children at home. Local authorities have a legal duty to check that home educators are complying with the law. If they are not satisfied they may issue a School Attendance Order which names the school your child should attend. If you breach the order, you can be fined up to £1,000.

It is the local authority or the governing body of the school that decides dates for school terms and holidays. Independent schools set term and holiday dates themselves.

What if your child fails to attend school regularly – or often arrives late?

You can be prosecuted. Some local authorities use a fast track process but usually you will receive a letter warning you that you may be prosecuted. You should be offered support, if needed, by the education welfare service but if your child's attendance fails to improve the authority can prosecute you under the Education Act 1996. Even if you try hard to get your child to turn up, you can be fined up to £1,000; however, the average fines are between £50 and £100 depending on your means. If you are found guilty, you would have a criminal record, which could affect your future employment.

If the authority thinks you have not done your best to make sure your child attends school, then you can be prosecuted for a more serious offence with higher penalties. The courts can make fines of up to £2,500 and send parents to prison for up to three months in these cases.

As said earlier, in 2003 the government introduced a package of measures to tackle the problem of parents who it felt were to blame for their children's poor attendance or poor behaviour at school. All three sanctions have since been extended to cover a wider range of situations so, for example, a child behaving badly at school does not need to have been excluded before parents can be subject to a parenting order or contract.

- **Parenting contracts:** Local authorities and schools can make contracts with parents to deal with their children's behaviour and school attendance. It is a two-sided agreement between you, the parent, and either the local authority or the governing body of a school. It is voluntary and so neither the parents nor the authority or school can be forced to make this sort of agreement. However, if the authority later prosecutes you for your child's truancy or applies for a parenting order (see below) it could tell the court if you refused to agree or keep to such a contract. Under such a contract, you agree to its terms; for example, that your child attends school regularly and punctually over a specified time period and the authority or governing body agrees to provide support. It can be used in cases of truancy, when a child's behaviour is becoming a problem, or when a pupil is excluded from school.

- **Parenting orders:** These are court orders which compel a parent to attend parenting classes as well as other demands required by the court for improving his child's behaviour. It is not a criminal conviction. It can be issued following a parent's conviction for his child's non-attendance, where his child has been excluded for serious misbehaviour either permanently or twice in 12 months for a fixed period, or where the child's behaviour is serious enough to have warranted a permanent exclusion. It is appropriate where parenting is considered a factor in the child's behaviour and the parents are unwilling to engage with the powers-that-be.

- **Penalty notices:** Local authorities (usually education welfare officers), senior school staff and the police may issue fines to parents for truancy and where an excluded child is in a public place during the first five days of the exclusion in school hours without reasonable excuse, such as a medical appointment.

  Penalty notices for non-attendance provide an alternative to prosecution and are fines (at the time of going to press, £50 if paid within 28 days). Parents who pay on time will not be prosecuted. However, if they do not pay the local authority will generally prosecute for the offence of irregular attendance under the Education Act 1996, section 444 (see above).

Your child's school disapproves of your plans for an extended holiday. Can it stop you?

Schools can authorise absence for holidays but generally the limit is ten school days. You should discuss proposed holidays with the school before you book them.

Heads may, in exceptional circumstances, give longer leave but any leave for holidays is entirely at the school's discretion, so it may depend on the reason you need extended leave.

Factors that they are likely to take into consideration include the time of year for the proposed trip (e.g. if it's close to exams), your child's attendance record, holidays already taken in the school year, the age and stage of education of your child, the ability of your child to catch up the work that they have missed and the reason why you are taking the time off during term time. The fact that you have a cheap flight on easyJet will not be persuasive, nor will the fact that you can only get the hotel that you want at that time.

If you take the holiday without the school's permission, you risk being fined or prosecuted. For one-off periods of unauthorised absence, fines are more common.

Playing truant

The New Labour government had as its target to slash truancy by one-third. However, as of August 2009 the rate of unauthorised non-attendance was one-third higher than in 1997. It was reckoned that on a typical day around 68,000 primary and secondary pupils skipped classes. It was reported (*Guardian*, 26 August 2009) that a parent was jailed every other week during term time for failing to prevent their child's truancy. There was also reported a substantial rise in the number made to sign parenting contracts. In 2008/09 the number of parenting contracts had gone up by 41 per cent to 6,861. The number of court-issued penalty notices went up by 12 per cent to 7,793.

Could your child be entitled to a free school lunch, or free milk?

Your child could qualify for free lunches if you receive certain welfare benefits such as Income Support, income-based Jobseeker's Allowance or Child Tax Credit. Local authorities must provide free lunches for those pupils who are eligible.

Back in 1971 it was Margaret Thatcher, then Secretary of State for Education, who withdrew free milk for the over-sevens. Her 1980 Education Act scrapped the obligation on the part of local authorities to provide school meals and scrapped compulsory nutritional standards (see below). Local authorities do not have to provide free milk but, if they do provide it, it must be free to those pupils eligible for free lunches. Under-fives are eligible for free milk under the Welfare Food Scheme, which ensures that youngsters from poor backgrounds receive basic levels of nutrition and is run by the Department of Health. There is a European subsidy allowing local authorities and schools to offer nursery and primary school pupils a maximum of 250ml of subsidised milk a day.

All four- to six-year-old children in state schools are also entitled to a free piece of fruit or vegetable each school day under the School Fruit and Vegetable Scheme, which is part of the Department of Health's 5 A DAY programme.

What can you do if you aren't happy about your child eating turkey twizzlers and pizzas at school?

Food provided by local authorities must meet national nutritional standards to provide a healthy and balanced diet. New standards, introduced in 2006, require:

- high-quality meat;
- at least two portions of fruit and vegetables with every meal; and
- bread, other cereals and potatoes regularly available.

Additionally, there are controls on other foods such as deep-fried food (no more than two portions per week) and fizzy drinks, crisps and chocolate, which should be banned from school meals or removed from vending machines.

The School Food Trust was established by the Department for Education and Skills in 2005 to 'transform school food and food skills, promote the education and health of children and young people and improve the quality of food in schools'.

What if you are concerned about the inappropriate behaviour of staff?

Discuss your concerns with the head teacher and, if still dissatisfied, the governing body and (if it is a community or voluntary-controlled school) the local authority too. If your complaint is about the head teacher, you will need to go straight to the governing body of the school.

If you are unhappy with the response, you can complain to the General

Teaching Council (GTC) if your complaint is about a teacher's misconduct. You cannot complain to the GTC about a teacher's competence – only the school or local authority can do this. The GTC publishes a guide on complaints for parents.

What if you are concerned about the school's health and safety record?

Serious incidents at school and on school journeys in the 1990s, in particular the Dunblane massacre of primary school children and the Lyme Bay canoe tragedy, resulted in new legislation and guidance covering school security and outdoor education. The Health and Safety at Work Act 1974 makes schools and local authorities responsible for the health and safety of their employees and anyone else on the premises – including pupils and visitors. Regulations made under the Act require employers to assess the risks to which they may be exposed and introduce measures to control those risks.

There must be a health and safety policy for the school, which should name the key person responsible for the policy implementation and development.

What is the school's responsibility if your child is injured on a school activity?

If your child is injured at school, the school would need to show that it had taken reasonable steps to avoid accidents. Any judgement about what is reasonable should take into account the regulations and official guidance covering health and safety, and any risks which the school should have anticipated.

The organisation of a safe system of supervision is primarily the duty of the head teacher. Legal cases often hinge on whether better supervision would have prevented an accident or whether it would have happened anyway. Generally schools are not responsible before and after school but where pupils are allowed into the grounds, there may be responsibility and liability. Prudent schools should ensure that school gates are not opened unless or until a member of staff is present in the playground to supervise activities.

... what about school trips?

Head teachers have a legal responsibility to ensure that there is a safe and reliable system of supervision of pupils in all authorised school activities, both on school premises in school hours and on school trips. Governors also share this legal responsibility as part of their overall responsibility for the conduct of the school. They should ensure that a risk assessment takes place before any school trip and that preventive and protective measures are considered. So this might mean increasing supervision for a particular group or changing the nature or type of activities undertaken to ensure no pupils are excluded because of a disability or cost.

The government recommends that supervision be considered as part of the risk assessment for the trip. There are no hard and fast rules about pupil:teacher ratios on trips but under normal circumstances it suggests that at least one teacher accompanies every six primary pupils and every 15 secondary aged pupils on local visits to museums, historical sites, etc. For trips involving swimming, overnight visits and trips abroad the recommended ratio is increased.

... what about school security?

A head teacher has the power to decide who may have access to school premises, and trespassers creating a nuisance or disturbance on school premises can be removed and prosecuted under the Education Act 1996. Schools are advised to work with local police to have appropriate security strategies in place, such as 'Keep Out' signs and CCTV cameras. Many primary schools will lock gates to prevent unwanted visitors and as a safeguard against children leaving the premises. A few secondary schools have adopted more stringent measures such as metal detectors to prevent weapons being brought into school. On rare occasions a head teacher may ban parents because of their conduct. However, in a 1999 court case about this issue (*Wandsworth v A*) the court said that parents should be given a written warning and the opportunity to put their case, however informally, before such a draconian action is taken.

Special educational needs

What does it mean for a child to have 'special educational needs'?

A child with special educational needs (SEN) should get help at school. A child has such needs if:

- they have significantly more difficulty learning than other children of the same age (because of literacy problems or behaviour problems);

    or

- they have a disability which restricts their use of educational facilities provided for children in their area.

In most cases schools decide what help to give children with learning difficulties.

School governing bodies have a legal responsibility under the Education Act 1996 to do their best to make sure children with SEN are identified and have their needs met. Primary and secondary schools provide help known as School Action and School Action Plus to provide extra support for children. At School Action, a child will receive help only from within the school's own resources; for example, extra help with reading for a dyslexic child or visual materials produced for children with communication difficulties. At School Action Plus, a child will receive additional help from outside the school. Local authorities generally provide this support, which can include advice for class teachers about classroom strategies, or individual help from a speech and language therapist or a specialist teacher.

If a child doesn't make enough progress on School Action Plus, or if it is obvious from the start that this level of help will be insufficient, the local authority will make a statutory assessment of the child. Your child's school (and you as a parent) also has a legal right to ask for this if it feels your child is not making good enough progress despite help from the school. If the local authority refuses, there is a right of appeal to a specialist tribunal – the first-tier tribunal (Special Educational Needs and Disability or SEND for short).

A statutory assessment involves a number of professionals who will observe, examine and report back on your child. The local authority educational psychologist may do specific tests and social services, health and school professionals will be consulted. Your views as a parent will also contribute to the assessment and you must be given the opportunity to either put in a written report or speak to a local authority officer. You can ask the local authority to contact professionals who know your child, and you can put in private reports you may have on your child. The local authority then decides on the basis of all the reports whether to go ahead and write a statement of special educational needs. This will describe your child's educational needs, the help they should get and the school they will attend. If the local authority decides against writing a statement, you have the right of appeal to SEND. You have no right of appeal if you disagree with a decision to make an assessment and to statement your child but you can make representations about this to the local authority. You also have the right to say which school you would like your child to go to.

The statement is a legal document and the educational help set out (in part 3 of the report) must be provided by law, so negotiating detailed and specific provision is important. It can include help from teachers and other professionals such as speech therapists and specialist teachers; programmes of help such as behaviour support or literacy support; equipment and specialist facilities; and support from a learning support assistant in class. If your child is being 'statemented', you should seek advice from parent partnership officers in your local area, or local and national voluntary organisations, to ensure the statement is the best it can be. There are further rights of appeal if you are unhappy with the provision set out in part 3 of the statement, or the description of needs in part 2 or the school named in part 4.

What can you do if you disagree with your child's statement of special educational needs?

The first-tier tribunal (SEND) hears appeals about local authority decisions and decides claims of disability discrimination against schools and local authorities. It cannot deal with complaints about the way help is provided or delays in drawing up a statement.

Complaints about how a school makes provision for help should generally go to the governing body of the school. Complaints about failure to carry out the help in a statement should be made to the local authority in the first instance but you may need to take advice if this does not resolve the problem. If you suffer delays and other problems with the statementing process itself, the Local Government Ombudsman may investigate your complaint but you must first complain directly to the local authority.

Playing a part in your child's schooling

What can you do if you want to play an active part in the running of your child's school?

You could consider becoming a school governor. Governors are volunteers who it is reckoned spend about six hours each month attending meetings and working.

Every school has a governing body. The governors are responsible to parents, funders and the community for making sure the school provides good quality education and promotes high standards of educational achievement. The governing body as a whole has legal responsibility for many aspects of school management without having to worry about being liable as individuals for any legal or financial problems the school may experience. Governors provide a strategic framework for the head teacher, who is responsible for day-to-day management of the school.

Depending on the type of school, governing bodies are made up of:

- parents elected by other parents;

- the head teacher, if the head wants to be a governor;

- teachers chosen by other teachers;

- non-teaching staff elected by other non-teaching staff;

- people appointed by the local authority;

- people chosen by governors from the local community; and

- people appointed by the church or foundation (in church and some other types of school).

If you become a parent governor, it is a voluntary role (so you won't be paid although expenses can be claimed). Schools welcome parents from different backgrounds (such as those with knowledge of the business world) as well as parents who can reflect the concerns of their local community. The commitment can be significant with meetings every term of the governing body and additional meetings if you sit on committees.

A few parent governors become parent governor representatives with speaking and voting rights on local authority committees dealing with education. Parent governor representatives speak for all parents in their area and form a national network, so that the individual representative can share with representatives in other areas the experience of working in – and with – their local authority. Their role is to hold their local authority to account and consult and feed back to parents on the local authority's discussions and decisions on education. Like parent governors in schools, their task is to represent parents, not to be mandated by them to act in a particular way or to be their delegate. Parent governor representatives don't get paid. They are elected from serving parent governors to represent the views of all parents on local authority committees dealing with education matters. Each local authority must appoint two and no more than five.

Since 2005, schools have no longer had to hold an annual parent meeting or publish an annual report, although some still do, but schools do have to consult parents on various issues; for example, when they review the school's behaviour policy and before an Ofsted inspection. Some schools provide opportunities for parents to have their voices heard, including setting up parent councils. This is a requirement of the new category trust schools, which choose a majority of trust members as their governors.

Problems with your school

What can you do if your child's school isn't up to scratch?

If you have concerns about the teaching in your child's school – whether this is the standard of teaching or the subjects taught – you have a legal right to complain to Ofsted, the inspection body. The inspectors won't look into complaints affecting your individual child, but they can bring forward an inspection if they think a school is generally not up to standard.

Problems affecting just your child should be raised first with the teachers and then the head teacher. If that doesn't resolve the matter, you can complain to the governing body. The local authority must also consider curriculum complaints. These can be about issues such as subjects taught, examination problems, charges for education and if a child is not being taught the National Curriculum.

What's the best way to handle a complaint with your school?

Most difficulties with schools are best resolved on a personal level with a meeting or phone call to the appropriate teacher. If something serious happens, such as your child being injured in an accident at school, being badly bullied or let down by the school, then you may have to make a formal complaint. In most cases this would be to the governing body of the school. Ask your school for a copy of its complaints procedure, which it must publish under the Education Act 2002.

Depending on the nature of the complaint, if you are dissatisfied with the governors' response, then you have a range of routes. New legislation is in the pipeline to expand the remit of the Local Government Ombudsman to hear complaints against schools.

Is it possible to take legal action against a school?

This should be the last resort. Even though parents are becoming more litigious, few claims against schools have been successful. In practice most claims are settled by insurance companies out of court. To win damages in court, parents have to establish that a school failed in a duty of care and that their child had suffered loss or injury as a result. Negligence cases include those involving children who have been bullied. Many claims have been unsuccessful but in a 2000 case involving a bullied schoolboy from Greater Manchester, the court ruled that the school had failed in its procedures and awarded damages of £1,500 for verbal bullying. However, it was found that teachers could not have foreseen that this would lead to a serious assault so no damages were awarded for physical injury.

Could your child sue a school or local authority for, for example, failing to diagnose their dyslexia and consequently harming their educational progress?

It is possible, although such cases are very rare. In July 2000 the House of Lords awarded Pamela Phelps £46,650 in damages from her local authority for negligence because her dyslexia was not diagnosed and she did not receive the special educational provision that she needed. Her condition was missed even though she was assessed by a local authority educational psychologist. She argued that after leaving school she had struggled to find the type of employment she had envisaged and, as a result, would suffer financially throughout her life.

CONTACTS

In the classroom

If you want more information on the National Curriculum and preparing for parents' evenings, see the Department for Children, Schools and Families (www.dcsf.gov.uk) and Ofsted (www.ofsted.gov.uk) websites.

Welfare

To find out more on discipline, complaints, special education, exclusions and attendance, see www.ace-ed.org.uk and www.childrenslegalcentre.com. For information on school lunches and diet, see the School Food Trust (www.schoolfoodtrust.org.uk).

To find out about the General Teaching Council, see www.gtce.org.uk.

For more information on dealing with bullying, see www.kidscape.org.uk.

Special educational needs

For information on special educational needs, see the Independent Panel for Special Education Advice (www.ipsea.org.uk).

Playing a part in your child's schooling

For information on becoming a school governor, see www.governorline.co.uk.

Problems

For information on dealing with problems at school, see
www.parentlineplus.org.uk, www.ace-ed.org.uk and
www.ofsted.gov.uk. To find a specialist lawyer, see www.clsdirect.org.uk

CHAPTER 6

Growing up: staying in and going out

The following two chapters deal with issues that concern parents as children grow up and gain their independence. This chapter is concerned with what can be broadly defined as child protection and health issues. It is arranged roughly chronologically, following children as they grow from babies totally dependent on your care, into young adults with private lives and sex lives. It is divided into three parts – staying in; going out; and, finally, health and sex.

Chapter 7 looks at the complementary aspects of young people growing up and becoming more responsible such as learning to manage money, starting jobs and eventually leaving home.

- **Staying in:** First, the chapter considers the issues that might arise as a result of leaving young children in the care of others or by themselves in your home. For example, we consider finding the right babysitter; the age at which it might be OK to leave your children 'home alone'; and then the disciplining of your children; for example, whether it is OK for you or another person to smack your child.

  Then we consider the influence that the media has on children – the time your child spends in front of the TV; the concept of broadcasting standards; what (if anything) does the '9 o'clock watershed' mean; and how DVDs, videos and video games are classified.

Finally, for this section we consider the increasing importance of new media and, in particular, the Internet and the increasingly important role it plays in our children's lives: what is your responsibility for you children safely using the Internet; and whether your children's downloading of music is illegal.

- **Going out:** The next section deals with the welfare of your child away from home and outside your control. It begins by looking at the law on child safety in cars and bikes.

  Then we consider the age at which your child can drink in a pub; what could happen if your underage child attempts to buy alcohol; restrictions on certain kinds of drinks such as 'alcopops' being marketed to the young; plus the age at which children can do various adult activities from buying cigarettes to getting a tattoo.

- **Health and sex:** This section starts by looking at whether your child can consent to medical treatment without your say-so and whether you have a right as a parent to be consulted on that advice. Finally, it looks at what age your child can have sex; whether your daughter can have an abortion without your permission; and the protections the law offers against sexual offences.

Staying in

How do you choose a babysitter?

See below for a guide on how to choose your babysitter. Having children look after other children, as many parents do, needs some sensible thought. Both the Royal Society for the Prevention of Accidents (ROSPA) and the National Society for the Prevention of Cruelty to Children (NSPCC) recommend that no one under 16 should be left to babysit. Parents can be prosecuted and fined if they leave their children in a situation which a court might judge to be 'neglectful'.

ROSPA is keen to point out that babysitting disasters are few and far between but it also says 'leaving children in the hands of other children increases the risk of harm being realised'. The group goes on to say that 'a lot of young people we spoke to, who were expected to look after younger brothers and sisters, felt trapped by their enforced child-minding duties and, in many cases, it had created a great deal of family tension ...some youngsters felt that they were being "blackmailed" into babysitting. A lot of the children felt "used".

Choosing a babysitter

When deciding to use a babysitter remember to:

- Follow your instincts. If in doubt, don't use them.

- Ask for at least two references and contact the referees yourself.

- Choose a babysitter over 16 years old.

- Listen to your child. Talk to them about any issue of babysitting that they are unhappy about.

- If your child is unhappy about your use of a particular babysitter, find someone else.

- Only use registered childminders. A list of local registered childminders can be found from your local authority children's information service.

Source: NSPCC

Some people find looking after children a responsibility, which is stressful and occasionally frustrating. ROSPA points out that the best babysitters have taken courses in child development and first aid, have experience sitting for others, and have support systems in place (e.g. their own parents would step in, in the event of a crisis or accident).

You should consider all eventualities before leaving your children in the hands of someone else, particularly someone under 16. Likewise, any prospective babysitter should be well prepared with enough information and know-how to be able to cope with most situations during the babysitting session.

If you decide to use a young babysitter (under 16), you must be prepared to take some responsibility for anything that should go wrong in your absence. ROSPA points out that you must also be prepared to take responsibility for the care and safety of your babysitter – so make arrangements for their safe return home and never let a young babysitter travel home alone late at night. It also recommends using some common sense if they want a friend to sit with them (same sex or opposite sex) noting that 'babysitting can be a lonely business'.

At what age is it OK to leave your children 'home alone'?

There is no easy answer. The law does not set a minimum age at which children can stay 'home alone'. However, it is an offence to leave a child alone when doing so puts them at risk.

So how do you know? The NSPCC recommends that you consider the following advice before leaving a child by himself:

- the child's age;

- the child's level of maturity and understanding;

- the place where your child will be left;

- how long the child will be left alone, and how often; and

- whether or not there are any other children alone with the child.

The NSPCC points out that babies or young children shouldn't be left 'home alone' (not even for a few minutes). Children under 13 years are regarded as not mature enough to cope with an emergency and so shouldn't be left alone for more than a very short period of time. Parents can be and are prosecuted by the police for wilful neglect if they leave a child unsupervised 'in a manner likely to cause unnecessary suffering or injury to health' (Children and Young Persons Act 1933).

If you do leave a child alone, remember to:

- leave a telephone number where you can be contacted and make sure you are available;

- talk to your child about keeping safe at home and point out potential dangers. Tell them not to answer the door to strangers;

- give clear instructions about what to do if there's an emergency. All children left alone should be able to phone the emergency services;

- leave a list of trusted people they can contact;

- put obvious dangers out of reach of children (medicines, chemicals, matches, etc.);
- make sure that the child is happy about being left;
- tell the child when you'll be back, and make sure you're back on time; and
- talk to him about the experience afterwards.

Source: NSPCC

Is it against the law to smack your child?

No, but as the NSPCC says, smacking is often a sign of a parent 'losing it'. While it is an offence for one person to assault another, when it comes to children parents may claim a defence of 'reasonable punishment' (under the Children Act 2004). By contrast, this defence is not open to parents in many European countries, where hitting children in any way is against the law. In England and Wales a parent could be prosecuted for assaulting a child if the hitting went beyond 'reasonable punishment'. However, the law does not define exactly what it means – it depends on the Crown Prosecution Service guidelines, which now state that assaults which, if committed against an adult, would be considered as 'common assault' leading to relatively minor injury are now to be considered as the more serious offence of actual bodily harm if the victim is a child. In Scotland the law is different and parents cannot hit a child under three; it is illegal to hit any child with an implement, to shake them or to hit them on the head. It is therefore still acceptable under UK law (with some variations) for parents to hit their children.

For those parents who draw the line between a 'harmless smack and physical abuse', the NSPCC points out that the UN Convention on the Rights of the Child (see chapter 1) and international human rights laws are clear that children should have equal protection under the law on assault, and that the use of physical punishment denies them their rights to physical integrity and human dignity. Further, as the group says, even seemingly inoffensive smacks can lead to unexpected injury, 'for example, ruptured eardrums, brain damage and injuries or even death from falls caused by blows'. The group adds, 'parents who use physical punishment may say they control the force of the smack and do not intend to harm their child but the reality is that adults usually resort to smacking when they are angry and have "lost it"'.

Are others (such as teachers, nursery workers and childcare workers) allowed to smack your child?

It is against the law for teachers, nursery workers and childcare workers to smack another person's child. But the NSPCC points out that anyone employed privately by a parent, such as a babysitter or nanny, may smack a child as long as the parent gives permission.

Should your children be watching this ...?

There has been much concern about a brewing 'crisis' in children's television and the poor quality of what's broadcast – an Ofcom review in 2007 found that just 1 per cent of children's programming comprised first-run UK-produced shows. The rest was either repeats or foreign programmes and mainly US cartoons. A series of phone-in scandals also shook confidence in the ethical standards of broadcasters. Ofcom, under the Communications Act 2003, can impose quotas on news and current affairs to protect quality standards and campaigners have made similar calls in relation to children's programming.

All UK TV channels – terrestrial and digital – as well as radio must conform to the media regulator, Ofcom's broadcasting code, which attempts to both set standards in relation to taste and decency, and contain protections relating to under-18-year-olds. According to the code, material that 'might seriously impair the physical, mental or moral development of people under 18 must not be broadcast' (section 1), plus there should be 'adequate protection' from 'harmful and/or offensive material' (section 2).

DVDs and videos are rated under the British Board of Film Classification system (BBFC) and are considered later in this chapter.

What is the 9 o'clock watershed, and how does it work?

It applies to TV. Programmes unsuitable for children should not, in general, be shown before 9pm or after 5.30am. On premium subscription film services, the watershed is 10pm. There is no watershed on premium subscription film services or pay per view services where there are security systems in place to protect youngsters, such as requirements for PIN numbers. Radio broadcasters should be conscious of times when children are particularly likely to be listening, such as the school run and breakfast time.

For TV programmes broadcast before the watershed or radio programmes broadcast when children are likely to be listening, clear information about content that may distress children should be given to the audience.

Shocked by what your children are watching, what should you expect?

The broadcasting code contains the following guidance, which ought to be followed:

- **Too many drugs?** The misuse of drugs, smoking and alcohol should not be featured in programmes made for children unless there is editorial justification and must not be 'condoned, encouraged or glamorised' in other programmes broadcast before the watershed or likely to be widely seen by under-18s (or when children are particularly likely to be listening on the radio) unless there is editorial justification.

- **Too violent?** Violence, after-effects and verbal descriptions, and dangerous behaviour 'easily imitable by children', must be limited in programmes broadcast before the watershed (or when children are particularly likely to be listening) and must also be justified by the context. There are also provisions relating directly to contentious issues such as suicide, self-harm as well as the occult.

- **Bad language?** The most offensive language should not be broadcast before the watershed or when children are particularly likely to be listening.

- **Sex?** Representations of sexual intercourse should not occur before the watershed (or when children are particularly likely to be listening) unless there is a serious educational purpose. Discussions on, or portrayal of, sexual behaviour must be editorially justified if included before the watershed, or when children are particularly likely to be listening. Nudity before the watershed must be justified by the context.

How does the film classification system work?

The film, DVD and video rating system should help parents make informed choices about the films their children should be watching (as well as the video and computer games they play – see later). It is illegal to supply a DVD, video or game with a BBFC age-rating to anyone under that age. Shop assistants can face criminal charges if they are caught supplying under-aged children. They can be fined and even imprisoned under the terms of the Video Recordings Act. It is the individual's responsibility and not the store's.

U – suitable for audiences aged four years and over ('U' stands for 'universal')

However, the BBFC notes that it 'is impossible to predict what might upset a particular child, especially at this lower end of the category range'. There used to be a category of Uc highlighting appropriate films for the very young but that category has been scrapped and DVDs now state: 'Particularly suited for young children'.

What about bad language? Only very mild (such as 'damn' and 'hell') but worse (such as 'bloody' or 'bugger') may be included 'where justified by the context'.

... sex? Not allowed – but characters may be seen kissing or cuddling and there may be references to sexual behaviour (i.e. to 'making love').

... violence? There might be brief fight scenes or moments where characters are placed in danger. However, 'moments of emotional stress or threat will be quickly resolved and the outcome will be reassuring'. There may be brief scary scenes and moments where the characters are placed in danger. As with violence, however, these scenes will be balanced by reassuring elements, such as comic interludes or music.

... drugs? Not normally, unless there is a very clear anti-drugs message which will be understood by a younger audience.

PG – suitable for general viewing but some scenes may be unsuitable for younger children ('PG' stands for 'parental guidance' which does not mean that a parent has to attend a viewing)

It should not disturb a child aged around eight or older. You need to consider whether the content might upset younger or more sensitive children. Such films aren't necessarily made for younger audiences. 'PG' works can explore 'challenging issues' such as domestic violence, bereavement or racism.

What about bad language? There may be mild bad language (such as 'shit' or 'son of a bitch') but 'context and delivery' are important.

... sex? References to sex are acceptable if the activity talked about or shown is implied and lacking in detail.

... violence? There should be no detail of violence so while there might be some blood, we would not see how the injury was inflicted.

... drugs? There might be innocuous or passing references to illegal drugs or drugs misuse although there should be no strong focus on this.

12A/12 – '12A' means that anyone aged 12 or over can go and see the film unaccompanied. Children younger than 12 may see the film if they are accompanied by an adult, who must watch the film with them. ('A' stands for 'accompanied' and 'advisory')

The BBFC says that it would never recommend taking a very young child to see a 12A film, though. The '12' certificate is just for videos, DVDs and games and '12A' is for films only. BBFC considers 12A films as suitable for children over the age of 12 and does not recommend taking a very young child to a 12A film. There is no lower age limit for a '12A' film and the BBFC says parents or guardians must decide whether the film is suitable for their child or children.

What about bad language? There may be strong language (e.g. 'fuck') but it must be infrequent.

... sex? References to sex may reflect what is familiar to most adolescents but should 'not go beyond what is suitable for them'. Sex should be 'brief and discreet'.

... violence? It shouldn't dwell on detail and there should be no emphasis on injuries or blood. However, in a horror context, occasional gory images may be allowed.

... drugs? There may be infrequent sights of drugs misuse but the portrayal should not be glamorised or provide instructional details.

15 – suitable only for 15 years and over

No one younger than 15 may see a '15' film in a cinema. No-one younger than 15 may rent or buy a '15'-rated video or DVD.

18 – suitable only for adults

No-one younger than 18 may see an '18' film in a cinema. No one younger than 18 may rent or buy an '18'-rated video.

R18 ('R' stands for restricted)

To be shown only in specially licensed cinemas, or supplied only in licensed sex shops, and to adults of not less than 18 years.

Subscription and pay per view services

No film refused classification by the BBFC should be broadcast on these services. BBFC 18-rated films must not be broadcast before 9pm on any service (except for pay per view services), and even then they may be unsuitable for broadcast at that time.

Premium subscription film services may broadcast up to BBFC 15-rated films or their equivalent, at any time of day provided there is a protection system (such as a PIN) before 8pm and after 5.30am restricting access to children. Pay per view services may broadcast up to BBFC 18-rated films or their equivalent, at any time of day provided there is a protection system pre-9pm and post-5.30am to restrict access to children. Premium subscription services and pay per view services may broadcast 'adult-sex' material between 10pm and 5.30am if there is a similar protection system in place.

Why are some films '12A' in the cinema but '15' on DVD?

The main reason for the difference is the content of the DVD 'add-ons', but occasionally these films will be marketed as being the 'uncut' edition or the 'extended' version of a film. This will mean that the works contain additional footage, either added to the film itself or included in the extras package, that have made the new version a '15'. Classification decisions may be stricter on video or DVD than at cinemas. This is because of the increased possibility of under-age viewing recognised at home.

Videos may be cut or classified more strictly than the same work for the cinema. It is more likely that a cinema audience has made a specific commitment to see a particular film, knows what to expect, and is therefore less likely to chance upon a film which they would regard as inappropriate. Plus, obviously, admission is regulated by age at the cinema entrance. The Video Recordings Act, by contrast, specifically requires the Board to take into account the likelihood that the video may be seen 'in the home'. The possibility that some viewers may be below the age for which the work was classified is clearly greater. Plus, viewers can use freeze-frame and rewind to watch scenes out of context.

What about video games? How are they classified?

Most video games are exempt from BBFC ratings – although at the time of going to press there is considerable pressure for a similar rating system to apply following the publication of a report in early 2008 by child psychologist Dr Tanya Byron, *Safer Children in a Digital World*. However, games are age rated under the voluntary system (run by the Pan-European Game Information). Games lose that exemption if they contain:

- sex;
- gross violence towards humans and animals;
- criminal activity; and
- drug use.

Should you let my children have access to the Internet?

Yes; but you also need to teach your children how to use the Internet safely and responsibly.

The *Safer Children in a Digital World* report proposed a comprehensive package of measures to protect children and young people from harmful and inappropriate material. Dr Byron found that while new technologies brought opportunities for children and young people, parents lacked confidence and awareness leaving their children vulnerable to risks.

The Internet has quickly assumed a key role in the lives of children – it is not just entertainment, but also an essential part of their education and, whether you like it or not, likely to be as central to their social lives as TV was to earlier generations. You should take time to learn how to protect your child because as the police agency, the Child Exploitation and Online Protection (CEOP) Centre, points out, 'where children go, child sex offenders will follow whether in the real or virtual world'.

CEOP says that child sex abusers find the Internet an easier place to make contact with children because of its anonymity. 'They will often lie and pretend to be younger than they are or people other than themselves,' the group says. 'They have been known to set up bogus email accounts and chat personas to mask their identity online.'

There are particular concerns around 'online grooming', defined as 'a course of conduct enacted by a suspected paedophile, which would give a reasonable person cause for concern that any meeting with a child arising from the conduct would be for unlawful purposes' (Sexual Offences Act 2003). Paedophiles often seek out young people looking for friends and use a number of 'grooming' techniques including building trust through lying, creating different personas and then attempting to engage the child in more intimate forms of communication. They will often use blackmail and guilt as methods of securing a meeting with the child.

According to CEOP, risks arise when young people give out their personal details to strangers, such as mobile numbers and pictures of themselves.

What can you do to protect your child online?

Your child needs to understand the importance of keeping their personal information personal. It is a good idea to ask them if they know how to block someone who they no longer wish to talk to. Consider creating some family rules which you will all agree to on online use, including not giving out personal information, or talking to strangers without discussing it. Remind your children that they should never meet up with someone that they have met online without you or another adult going with them.

CEOP advises that if you are concerned that your child may be at risk, it may be necessary to log or monitor their conversations, and this can be done through some forms of filtering software – but this should be considered carefully, since a child may feel that they have to hide more from their parents if they think they are not trusted. GetNetWise has lists of filtering and monitoring software. If you think your child may be in touch with an adult online, make a report or call 999 if they are at immediate risk.

How to protect your children in social networking areas:

- Encourage them only to upload pictures that you as their parents would be happy to see – anything too sexy to be passed round the dinner table should not make it on to the web. It is also not a good idea to post pictures which can identify your children's school.

- Tell your children not to post their phone number or email address on their homepage.

- Help your children to adjust their account settings so that only approved friends can instant message them.

- Check that your children have ticked the 'no picture forwarding' option on their social networking site settings page – this will stop people sending pictures from their page around the world without their consent.

- Encourage them not to give too much away in a blog. Friends can call them for the address of the latest party rather than read about it on their site.

- Ask them to show you how to use a social networking site.

How to make sure your children are safe online:

- Know what your children are doing online and who they are talking to. Ask them to teach you to use any applications you have never used.

- Help your children to understand that they should never give out personal details to online friends – personal information includes their messenger ID, email address, mobile number and any pictures of themselves, their family or friends. If your child publishes a picture or video online, anyone can change it or share it.

- If your children receive spam/junk email and texts, remind them never to believe them, reply to them or use them.

- It's not a good idea for your children to open files that are from people they don't know. They won't know what they contain – it could be a virus, or worse – an inappropriate image or film.

- Help your children to understand that some people lie online and that therefore it's better to keep online mates online. They should never meet up with any strangers without an adult they trust.

- Always keep communication open for children to know that it's never too late to tell someone if something makes them feel uncomfortable.

- Teach young people how to block someone online and how to report them if they feel uncomfortable.

Your children are downloading their music from the Internet. Is this illegal?

It could be. Illegal downloading is rife, particularly amongst the young. According to research by the International Federation of the Phonographic Industry and analyst Jupiter Research, only one in 20 downloads is actually paid for.

The Internet has made it easy to share tunes through online services that offer file-sharing or peer-to-peer (P2P). Each file-sharing network is a little different but basically a would-be file-sharer goes to a website and downloads its software. Usually the software creates a 'shared media' folder on your computer, which opens it up to fellow file-sharers. This enables you to exchange photos and videos, as well as music, software and games, directly between your computer and theirs. It is illegal to share music and film unless you created the work.

The music industry body, the British Phonographic Industry (BPI), has guidance for parents on its website.

File-sharers have been sued by the recording and film industries and some paid big fines. Generally speaking, the UK music industry has taken a 'gently, gently' approach since 2004 when the BPI launched 150 cases, most of which settled for around £2,000. It has been quiet compared to the more gung-ho approach of the Americans, where more than 20,000 lawsuits have been brought since 2004. In early 2008 one 30-year-old single mother who allegedly had 24 songs that were available for download was forced to pay $9,250 per song. A spokesman for the BPI says that it has refused to rule legal actions out completely 'but in real terms we simply don't believe that this is a proportionate response'. 'Not to mention that it would cost millions of pounds and clog up the courts for years,' he adds.

While there is no problem if you are sharing the content that you have originally created yourself, nearly all music and film files on file-sharing services are protected by copyright, and therefore people uploading (sending) them run legal risks. Parents have been held legally liable when the family computer has been used to break the law, even if they were not themselves engaged in illegal activity.

If you are concerned that your children are downloading music illegally ...

- Get your children to show you how they are using the computer and what they are sharing.

- Check your computer. You can make sure you are aware of what is on your family computer – whether you or another member of the household put it there. There is free information available that will take you through how to identify or disable P2P software step-by-step (e.g. www.ifpi.org).

- It is also important to make sure that your computer is protected against viruses and spyware and has firewall software installed.

- As a rule of thumb, if the music is free, it's likely to be illegal.

Can your child be sued for downloading?

Not if he has downloaded songs that have been put online with the approval of record labels and artists – which usually involves paying for royalties. There is a huge and growing range of download services such as iTunes and Amazon, subscription services (e.g. Napster, eMusic, Comes with Music, etc.), Internet radio (e.g. last.fm) and online streaming services (e.g. We7 and Spotify).

The BPI says it cannot differentiate between children and adults in its legal actions because it does not actually know their identities. The BPI has asked Internet companies to urge their customers who are caught stealing music online to stop, but says so far the Internet companies have refused. Instead, the BPI has to go to court to force Internet service providers to hand over personal information, which is usually the parent's. But if it is a child uploading music, then the BPI says it could still pursue legal action if the parent refused liability.

You are shocked by the high sexual content of the teen magazines your daughter reads. What can you do?

There has been public concern about the overtly sexual content of teenage magazines. Many parents feel that teen mags set a poor example. In a study of 3,200 young women carried out in 2007 by Girlguiding UK, over half of 16- to 25-year-olds said the media made them feel that 'being pretty and thin' was the 'most important thing'. A quarter of girls aged between 10 and 15 said the same. The most influential role models by far (cited by 95 per cent of girls) were Kate Moss and Victoria Beckham, both of whom are famously thin. A report in the *Sunday Telegraph* (15 March 2009) which reviewed several magazines aimed at teenage girls found that they contained 'sexually-explicit material that was potentially in breach of the industry's editorial code'. One magazine *Bliss*, whose readers have an average age of 15, featured on the front of its then current issue the coverlines: 'The Sex Factor, your questions answered' and 'Gang raped – for a mobile phone'.

The publishing industry, working with the Home Office, has developed guidelines on how teenage magazines should handle sexual subject matter. The Teenage Magazine Arbitration Panel was set up in 1996 with guidelines for magazines where 25 per cent or more of the readership are young women under the age of 15. The panel will consider complaints from the public. It says that it has 'no firm evidence to suggest that appropriate, professional advice in teenage magazines encourages people to enter into sexual relationships'. But it adds, 'the UK's depressing record of the highest teenage pregnancy rate in Europe shows that British adolescents need high quality information and guidance on issues of sexual health and relationships'.

The body has been criticised for inaction. In 2005 it upheld its first complaint in more than seven years. It decided an article about prostitution in Zambia featured in an issue of *Sugar* 'should have directly referred to underage sex being illegal in the UK'.

Going out

Does your child need a car seat?

It depends on the age and build of your child. The law requires all children travelling in cars to use the right child seat (or restraint) until they are either 12 years old or 135cm in height, whichever comes first. After this they must use an adult seat belt. ROSPA has a website with full details. Choose a seat that is suitable for your child's weight and height, ROSPA recommends. Babies need to be in rearward-facing baby seats and ROSPA recommends you wait until they weigh 13kg or outgrow the seat (check the manufacturer's instructions for how to spot this) and can sit up unaided before you move them to a forward-facing seat.

It is the driver's responsibility to ensure that children under the age of 14 years are seated correctly in accordance with the law – see box.

Child car seats

Children up to three years old

- In the front seat, the child must use the correct child restraint (in other words, one appropriate for your child's weight and height). It is illegal to carry a child in a rear-facing child seat in the front which is protected by an active frontal airbag.

- In the rear seat, the child must use the correct child restraint.

- In a licensed taxi or licensed private hire car, if a child restraint is not available then the child may travel unrestrained in the rear. This is the only exception for children under three years, and has been introduced for practical rather than safety reasons.

Children aged three and above until they reach their 12th birthday or 135cm in height:

- In the front seat, the child must use the appropriate child restraint (in other words, one appropriate for your child's weight, size and age).

- In the rear seat, the child must use the appropriate restraint where seat belts are fitted. There are three exceptions where there is no child seat available. In each case the child must use the adult belt:

    (i)   in a licensed taxi or private hire vehicle;

    (ii)   if the child is travelling a short distance for reason of unexpected necessity;

    (iii) if there are two occupied child restraints in the rear which prevent the fitment of a third.

- In addition, a child three years and over may travel unrestrained in the rear seat of a vehicle if seat belts are not fitted.

Children over 135cm in height, or who are 12 or 13 years old:

- In the front seat, the adult seat belt must be worn if available.

- In the rear seat, the adult seat belt must be worn if available.

Passengers over 14 years old:

- When travelling in the front or rear seat, an adult seat belt must be worn if available.

Other vehicles such as vans, buses, coaches, minibuses and goods vehicles:

- In the front seat, the law requires children (and adults) travelling in the front of all vehicles, including vans, buses, coaches, minibuses and goods vehicles, to use an appropriate child restraint or adult seat belt.

- In the rear seats of small minibuses, passengers sitting in the rear of minibuses that have an unladen weight of 2,540kg or less must wear the seat belts that are provided. It is the driver's responsibility to ensure that:

  (i) children under 3 years of age use an appropriate child restraint if available;

  (ii) children aged between 3 and 11 years, under 135cm tall, use an appropriate child restraint if available, or if not available, wear the seat belt, if available;

  (iii) children aged 12 and 13 years (and younger children who are 135cm or taller) use the seat belt, if available.

  Passengers over the age of 14 years in smaller minibuses are legally responsible for wearing a seat belt themselves.

- In the rear seats of larger minibuses, passengers over the age of 14 must wear seat belts (over 2,540kg unladen weight). However, all passengers are strongly advised to wear seat belts or use the correct child seat on all journeys.

- In the rear seats of coaches, passengers over the age of 14 must wear seat belts. However, all passengers are strongly advised to wear seat belts or the correct child seat on all journeys.

If you are convicted of failing to wear a seat belt as a driver or passenger, you could face a fine of up to £500. As a driver, if you are convicted of failing to ensure that a child passenger (under the age of 14 years) is using an appropriate child restraint or wearing a seat belt according to the legal requirements described above, you could also face a fine of up to £500.

In addition to the legal penalties, failure to wear a seat belt or failure to ensure that a child passenger uses an appropriate child restraint or wears a seat belt according to the legal requirements described above, could affect any claims against your motor insurance cover.

You could also face civil proceedings for damages, if (for example) you failed to safely carry someone else's child. But, as ROSPA notes, the most serious penalty of all could be that you or a passenger loses their life.

What happens if there are more passengers than seat belts?

The Department for Transport states (on its Think! Road Safety website) that the law 'doesn't prevent you from carrying more adult passengers than there are seat belts … However, children up to 135cm tall must use child restraints with few exceptions, which means they must use the seats in the vehicle that have seat belts to secure their restraints. That can limit carrying capacity.' The advice goes on to say that 'the way in which passengers are carried must not cause danger to any person in the vehicle, for instance by overloading with unbelted passengers. Adult passengers without a seat belt can injure others in an accident. The police can prosecute if they judge that an unbelted passenger is a risk to the others in the vehicle.'

ROSPA takes the view that carrying more passengers than there are seat belts is not safe, and points out that between eight and 15 front seat occupants are killed every year by unbelted rear seat passengers flying forwards in an accident.

How do you find the right child seat for your bike?

Again ROSPA has an extensive guide on its website and advises parents to use special child seats available from good cycle dealers and childcare shops that conform to *BS EN 14344:2004*, the British Standard for Child Seats for Cycles. Such seats are designed to carry children who are between 9kg and 22kg (roughly nine months to five years).

Your child is going on a trip organised by someone else – for example, a school or a club. What level of care can you expect?

The standard that must be fulfilled for any adult taking care of your child is that of a reasonably careful parent who has some experience of the activity to be undertaken. They cannot be held liable for pure accidents but only for negligence. Negligence means taking actions or failing to act in a way which is likely to cause injury to someone and that they should have had that outcome in their contemplation if they had stopped to think about it.

By law, no one can escape the responsibility for causing personal injury or death just by obtaining a signed disclaimer. However, if the consent form alerts you to risks which you are not happy with, make further enquiries before allowing your child to participate.

Central to the whole process of ensuring safety for children engaged in adventure activities is a formal risk assessment process. Warnings of risk should be adequate, equipment should be in good order and proper instructions should be given as to use of equipment or facilities. You can check what insurance cover is available to cover the activity, should there need to be a claim. ROSPA recommends that parents should be told not only what their child will be doing, but also information about the skills of the supervisors before embarking on a trip. If you are unsure about safety at a particular facility, you could check with the Adventure Activities Licensing or with ROSPA.

What about playgrounds?

Unless there are specific warning signs, playgrounds should be designed for child play without adult supervision. Those responsible for building the playground should have complied with advisory standards and codes of practice covering safe play equipment. Other risky activities that require proper supervision need to also abide by appropriate ratios of children to carers (e.g. a bouncy castle). For further information, see the website of the Child Accident Prevention Trust, the Health & Safety Executive or ROSPA.

What if you are going abroad?

If you are booking a family holiday abroad and hope to take part in some adventure activities while you are away, you need to be extra-careful about the safety standards. If the activities are booked as part of a package holiday (package means a prearranged combination of at least two items –

transport, accommodation, or other tourist services not ancillary to transport or to accommodation which account for a significant proportion of the package), you have a level of protection if something does go wrong. The organiser will be liable if the package goes wrong ,which means a claim can be brought at home in England.

If a tour operator states that a holiday is suitable 'for children' but then, for example, access to facilities is very poor for children who are still in prams or buggies, a claim can be made against the operator. This claim can be made if there has been a misrepresentation to you about those facilities that will be offered which has been relied on and causes the accident. Tour operators may also be liable for failures not only of their own employees ,but also for failures by suppliers of services that they use in the country you are visiting. Therefore, a claim can be made against a tour operator for accidents that occurred, while carrying out activities with local services in the country you are visiting. However, if these activities are not booked in the UK as part of a package then it will be down to local laws.

What if there are accidents involving animals?

All owners of animals should take reasonable care to prevent animals causing harm. Keepers of animals are not responsible, in the absence of negligence, for any injury if the animal is not of 'a dangerous species' (as defined by law) unless the damage caused was likely to be severe or likely to happen if the animal was not restrained, the likelihood of the harm was caused by the abnormal characteristics of that particular animal or its unusual response to particular situations, and the keeper of the animal knew the animal had those dangerous characteristics. If the animal belongs to a dangerous species, a claim should succeed unless the other side can prove he acted responsibly. There are specific criminal sanctions for dangerous dogs (e.g. pit bull terriers or types bred for fighting).

At what age can your child start driving?

Different vehicles have different minimum ages and restrictions. Before your child can drive though, they must hold a provisional driving licence and ensure that their vehicle is roadworthy, taxed and insured. If your child is learning to drive, they must go out with a driver who is over 21 years with a licence. The learner must have 'L' plates. There is more information on the Directgov website.

Learners now have to take a theory test as well as a practical driving test. Your child can take their driving theory test once their provisional licence becomes valid – for car drivers the earliest date is normally when they turn 17 (although they apply for the licence up to three months before). (If you are disabled and receiving disability living allowance, you can apply when you are 16.)

If your child wants to ride a moped, he can take the theory test when he is 16, but again you must make sure he has a valid provisional licence.

New drivers should remember that they are effectively 'on probation' for the first two years of their driving life. Your child's licence will be revoked if they build up six or more penalty points within two years of passing their first driving test. They will need to reapply for their driving licence as a learner driver and re-sit their driving test.

More generally, parents need to educate their children as to the dangers that they as inexperienced drivers pose to both themselves and others. The figures record that drivers are most at risk of having an accident in the first two years or so after they pass their test. There are some sobering statistics. As many as 20 per cent of newly qualified drivers have a crash of some description within a year. Around 16 per cent more drivers aged 16 to 19 are killed now compared with 15 years ago.

We look at driving under the influence of drink and drugs below. There is more information on the Department for Transport's Think! campaign site.

At what age can your child drink or go into a pub?

Unsurprisingly, the law very carefully prescribes the extent to which young people can drink. However, the law doesn't exist to provide a guide for parents. In 2009 the Chief Medical Officer, Sir Liam Donaldson offered parents just such advice (in a document called *Guidance on the Consumption of Alcohol by Children and Young People*). His view was that 'an alcohol-free childhood' was 'the healthiest and best option'.

In particular, Donaldson recommended:

- if children drink alcohol, it shouldn't be before they reach 15 years;

- for those aged 15 to 17 years old, alcohol consumption should 'always be with the guidance of a parent or carer, or in a supervised environment';

- parents and young people should be aware that drinking at any age can be hazardous to health; and

- if young people aged 15 to 17 consume alcohol, it should be 'infrequently and certainly no more than once a week'.

Young people can go to the pub at any age. Children can go into any part of a pub as long as you accompany them and they can have soft drinks (although some pubs have restrictions on their licences). More generally, young people's access to alcohol is closely prescribed especially for the very young and so:

- **Under-5s:** It is against the law to give an alcoholic drink to a child under 5 (except under medical supervision) – the age is 14 years in Northern Ireland.

- **Under-16s:** They can go into any part of a pub as long as you accompany them and they can have soft drinks (however some pubs have restrictions on their licences).

- **Over-16s:** They can drink beer, wine or cider with a meal if it is bought by an adult and they are accompanied by an adult (but not spirits).

- **Under 18s:** It is against the law for anyone under 18 to buy alcohol in a pub, off-licence, supermarket or other outlet, or for anyone to buy alcohol for someone under 18 to consume in a pub or a public place.

- **Over-18s:** They can buy and drink alcohol legally in licensed premises in Britain.

Young people going to a pub by themselves may well be asked to prove that they are 18 or older. Pubs accept the following forms of proof of age:

- photocard driving licence;

- passport; and

- proof of age card.

For more information and to find out about the UK's national guarantee scheme for proof-of-age cards visit the Proof of Age Standards Scheme website.

What could happen if your under-age child attempts to buy alcohol?

The police might impose an on-the-spot fine, confiscate the drink, and contact you as parent. If an adult buys alcohol for your child, again the police can demand an on-the-spot fine from the adult and if that adult is working in a shop or a pub and they offend again, they may have to go to court where they can be fined and even lose their alcohol licence.

What is the law relating to drink-driving?

It is an offence to drive with more than 80 milligrams of alcohol in 100ml of blood, or 35 micrograms of alcohol in 100ml of breath. But the Department of Transport warns against translating those measures into units saying, 'you can't calculate your alcohol limit, so don't try'.

The maximum penalty for causing death by careless driving while under the influence of drink or drugs is 14 years' imprisonment, disqualification for at least 2 years and a mandatory extended driving test, and for driving while over the limit the maximum penalty is 6 months' imprisonment, a fine of up to £5,000 and disqualification for up to 12 months and 3 years if convicted twice in the last 10 years. According to the Department for Transport, if you drive at twice the legal alcohol limit you are at least 30 times more likely to cause a road crash, than a driver who hasn't.

The government launched a campaign in 2009 aimed at young people, warning of the dangers of 'drug-driving' – it is reckoned that one in five drivers killed in road accidents might have drugs in their system. Research by the Department for Transport shows that one in ten young male drivers reported being under the influence of drugs while driving. Anyone convicted of driving while on drugs will get a minimum 12-month ban, a criminal record and fine. In terms of testing, there are no legal limits – except of course any use of illegal drugs is against the law. As opposed to the breathalyser test, the police rely on physical tests to determine competence such as measuring pupil dilation, being asked to count (cannabis and heroin slow users down and cocaine speeds it up) or walk a line.

Are there any restrictions on 'alcopops' being marketed to young people?

There is industry self-regulation which seeks to limit the worst excesses of the drinks industry. Since the mid-1990s there have been successive calls for a crackdown on alcohol advertising in particular concerning campaigns for 'alcopops' seeking to glamorise drinking, target the young and encourage binge drinking.

In September 2009 the British Medical Association called for all alcohol advertising, including sport and music sponsorship, to be banned to discourage young people from taking advantage of cheap drinks promotions. The BMA report, *Under the Influence*, described Britain as being 'awash with pro-alcohol messaging, marketing and behaviour'.

The Portman Group, the industry-funded group that promotes sensible drinking, introduced a code of practice on the naming, packaging and promotion of drinks in 1996 to ensure that drinks are marketed in 'a socially responsible way and to an adult audience only'. The code has its own independent complaints system and if a product is found in breach of the code, a 'retailer alert bulletin' is issued asking retailers not to stock the offending product unless and until it has been amended to comply with the code. The fourth edition of the code of practice (which came into force in January 2008) disallows:

- particular appeal to under-18s;
- confusion as to the product's alcoholic nature;
- emphasis on alcoholic strength;
- association with 'bravado... dangerous or anti-social behaviour';
- association with 'sexual success';
- any link to 'illegal, irresponsible or immoderate consumption';

- urging consumers to 'drink rapidly or "down" their drinks in one';
- suggestion that drinking can lead to 'social success or popularity'; and
- claims that the product can 'enhance mental or physical capabilities'.

It was found in April 2008 that almost one-quarter of alcopop brands were appearing to fail to comply with the Portman Group's code. If you have concerns about a particular drink, you can contact the Portman Group. Its website has details about its complaints procedure.

Your son complains that he has been thrown out of a nightclub. What standards of conduct can you expect from bouncers?

Since 2003 bouncers (or door supervisors) have to be licensed and regulated by the watchdog Security Industry Authority (under the Private Security Industry Act 2001). They now have to pass a criminal background check, display effective communication skills as well as reach set levels of training and professional standards. Security at pubs or nightclubs should have identity cards with their details and a photograph clearly on display – if their ID is not visible they are likely to be working illegally. It is a criminal offence to work in these sectors without a licence.

The National Certificate for Door Supervisors takes four or five days to achieve and covers conflict management as well as dealing with awkward situations. Door supervisors are expected to ban people who are drunk, under the influence of drugs, have a reputation for criminal or bad behaviour or who exhibit aggressive behaviour, explains Steve Dennis, head of business development at the BIIAB (which provides training for the certificate). They are also there to make sure people conform to any dress code and that clubs and pubs stick to limits for the number of people on premises. They also monitor behaviour inside and deal with those who threaten others' safety, spoil their enjoyment, put the venue's licence at risk, and, when it comes to closing time, ensure that people finish drinks promptly.

Steve Dennis adds that their role is 'not just throwing people out but defusing potentially dangerous situations without using force'. Any physical intervention 'has to be reasonable', he argues. 'The aim is to avoid problems rather than employing strong-arm tactics. Door supervisors should only employ force as the very last resort – and then it should only be a reasonable amount.' This approach is supported by the Security Industry Authority's Code of Conduct and is covered within the training they receive as part of their qualification for their licence.

If the dispute is about age, then it is up to the individual to demonstrate that they are old enough. If the person cannot provide proof, they shouldn't let them in – that's part of the code.

If parents are concerned about the conduct of security staff, they can go to the nightclub or pub concerned, the security company that employs the bouncer or the Security Industry Authority.

How old does your child have to be to get a tattoo?

18 years old – see box.

How old do you have to be?

There are various age-related restrictions – see table.

Age-restricted sales list of products	Age (years)
Alcohol	18
Solvents	18
Lighter fuel	18
Knives, blades and axes	16
Tattooing	18
Fireworks	18
Cigarettes and tobacco	18
Air guns and pellets	17
National Lottery and Instant scratch card tickets	16
Chocolate liqueurs	16
Aerosol spray paints	16
Petrol	16

Health and sex

Can your child consent to medical treatment without your say-so?

Adults are usually regarded as competent to decide their own course of medical treatment. There is also a right to consent to treatment for anyone aged 16 to 18 (Family Law Reform Act 1969).

Young people under the age of 16 can consent to medical treatment if they have sufficient maturity and judgement. This was clarified by the House of Lords in the case of *Gillick* – see chapter 5 for a discussion of that case. Although it is an offence to have sex with someone under the age of 16 (see later), it is lawful for doctors to provide contraceptive advice and treatment without parental consent providing certain criteria are met. These criteria, known as the Fraser Guidelines, were laid down by Lord Fraser in *Gillick* and require the professional to be satisfied that:

- the young person will understand the professional's advice;
- they cannot be persuaded to inform their parents;
- they are likely to begin, or to continue, having sex with or without contraceptive treatment;
- unless they receive contraceptive treatment, their physical or mental health, or both, are likely to suffer;
- their best interests require them to receive contraceptive advice or treatment with or without parental consent.

Although these criteria specifically refer to contraception, the principles are deemed to apply to other treatments, including abortion (see later).

Young people under the age of 16 have as great a right to confidentiality as any other patient. If someone under 16 is not judged mature enough to consent to treatment, the consultation itself can still remain confidential.

The judgment in the House of Lords referred specifically to doctors but it is considered to apply to other health professionals, including nurses. It might also be interpreted as covering youth workers and health promotion workers who may be giving contraceptive advice and condoms to young people under 16, but this has not been tested in court.

If a person under the age of 18 refuses to consent to a course of medical treatment, it is possible in some cases for their parents or the courts to overrule their decision. However, this right can only be exercised on the basis that the welfare of the young person is paramount. In this context 'welfare' does not simply mean their physical health. The psychological effect of having the decision overruled would have to be taken into account and would normally only be an option when the young person was thought likely to suffer 'grave and irreversible mental or physical harm'. Usually when a parent wants to overrule a young person's decision to refuse treatment, health professionals will apply to the courts for a final decision.

Do you have a right as a parent to be consulted on medical advice given to your child?

There is no Act of Parliament that defines when a confidential relationship arises with respect to your child and medical advice. However, the courts have recognised the concept of confidentiality and legal action can be taken if confidential information is disclosed or misused.

The professional codes of practice of doctors, nurses and other health professionals place a duty on them not to disclose information about individual patients without their consent, except in exceptional circumstances.

The duty of confidentiality owed to a person under 16 is the same as that owed to any other person. Even if the health professional does not consider that a young person has sufficient understanding to consent to treatment, the consultation can remain confidential.

Exceptional situations may occur where a professional believes the health, safety or welfare of the patient or others is at grave risk. It would be usual to counsel the person to try to get them to agree to pass information on. If the patient will not agree to this, the decision whether to disclose information in these circumstances would depend on the degree of current or potential harm. It does not depend on the age of the patient.

The principle of confidentiality is not changed by guidance in England on working with sexually active young people published in the revised version of *Working Together to Safeguard Children from Harm* (DfES, 2006). The guidance states that, in making decisions about whether to share information about a young person with social services, the child's best interests must be the overriding consideration. Decisions should always be based on an assessment of that individual's situation and professionals have discretion to make decisions on a case-by-case basis taking account of a range of factors. This applies to all young people, including those under the age of 13. The guidance does state that cases involving under-13s should always be discussed with a nominated child protection worker in the practitioner's organisation. However, it clearly indicates that professionals have the discretion not to refer a young person to other agencies where this would not be in their best interest.

At what age can your child have sex?

From January 2001 the age of consent became equal for all – gay men, lesbians and heterosexuals. The age of consent is 16 years in England, Wales and Scotland, and (as of June 2008) Northern Ireland. The age of consent has shifted over the years reflecting changing social mores. In 1967 when gay sex was partially decriminalised, the age of consent for gay men was set at 21 (16 for heterosexuals) and there was no age of consent relating to lesbians.

Can your 15-year-old daughter have an abortion without your say-so?

If your daughter is under 16 years and needs an abortion, doctors will encourage her to involve you, or another adult, in that decision. In rare cases when parents can't be involved, an under-16-year-old can have an abortion without her parents' knowledge, as long as two doctors believe that it is in her best interests, and that she fully understands what is involved. If she has an abortion, she has the right for it to remain confidential, regardless of age, unless there are serious child protection concerns in which case the healthcare professional can consider whether other agencies need to be informed.

The Abortion Act 1967 sets out the legal framework and allows termination of pregnancy subject to conditions. Under the Abortion Act, abortions must be performed by a doctor in a premises approved by the

Secretary of State for Health. Nurses can be involved in abortion treatment under the supervision of a doctor, but do not work entirely independently.

When can an abortion be performed?

An abortion can be performed provided that two doctors agree in good faith that one or more of the following grounds for treatment are met:

1. the continuance of the pregnancy would involve risk to the life of the pregnant woman greater than if the pregnancy was terminated;

2. the termination is necessary to prevent grave permanent injury to the physical or mental health of the pregnant woman;

3. the continuance of the pregnancy would involve risk, greater than if the pregnancy was terminated, of injury to the physical or mental health of the pregnant woman;

4. the continuance of the pregnancy would involve risk, greater than if the pregnancy was terminated, of injury to the physical or mental health of any existing child(ren) of the family of the pregnant woman;

5. there is a substantial risk that if the child was born it would suffer from such physical or mental abnormalities as to have serious disabilities; or in an emergency, certified by the operating practitioner, as immediately necessary:

    (i)   to save the life of the pregnant woman; or

    (ii) to prevent grave permanent injury to the physical or mental health of the pregnant woman.

In relation to grounds 3 and 4, the doctor may take account of the pregnant woman's actual or reasonably foreseeable environment, including social and economic circumstances. Most abortions of unwanted pregnancies are carried out under those grounds.

As abortions in developed countries are up to ten times safer than going through the later stages of pregnancy and birth, doctors argue that for most women having an abortion is safer than birth. In practice abortion treatment is relatively freely available to women in England and Wales, although it is not available 'on demand' (in other words, the above 'grounds' or criteria have to be met). Due to recent better funding of abortion by the National Health Service (NHS), a greater proportion of abortions are taking place at an earlier stage in gestation in the UK.

In England and Wales abortion is legal up to the 24th week of pregnancy, and in some rare circumstances after this date. In 2005, in England and Wales, 89 per cent of abortions were carried out at under 13 weeks' gestation and 67 per cent were at under 10 weeks in the UK. It was also found that 84 per cent of abortions were funded by the NHS (just over half (52 per cent) of that number took place in the independent sector but under NHS contract). As a minimum standard, no woman should need to wait longer than 3 weeks from her initial referral to the time of her abortion. A small minority of GPs won't refer patients to get abortion treatment or give abortion advice because they don't agree with abortion. The regulatory body, the General Medical Council says if a doctor doesn't want to discuss abortion, they must promptly refer the woman to a doctor who can do so. Doctors are not required to advertise their views in advance, and so for impartial abortion advice or referral, you can check the Department of Health's registry of approved Pregnancy Advice Bureaux. Many of these can be used for free on the NHS.

What protections does the law offer against sexual offences?

In England, Wales and Northern Ireland the same laws apply to heterosexual and homosexual activity and offences can be committed by anyone, male or female, over the age of 10 years, the age of criminal responsibility – see chapter 8 for a discussion of criminal responsibility and young people.

It is an offence to intentionally engage in sexual touching with a young person aged 13, 14 or 15. This covers all physical contact, including touching with any part of the body, with anything else and through anything, for example, through clothing. It includes penetration.

Technically, a teenage fumble behind the bike sheds (not just intercourse but kissing) is a crime between under-16-year-olds, although the Crown Prosecution Service is unlikely to prosecute young people of a similar age having consensual sex. Its guidance specifies that it is 'not in the public interest to prosecute children who are of the same or similar age and understanding that engage in sexual activity, where the activity is truly consensual for both parties and there are no aggravating features, such as coercion or corruption'. The CPS goes on to say that in such cases protection would 'normally be best achieved by providing education for the children and young people and providing them and their families with access to advisory and counselling services'.

However, a person aged 18 years or over can be convicted for the above crime and is liable to up to 14 years' imprisonment. A person under the age of 18 is liable to up to 5 years' imprisonment. A person may claim in their defence that they believed the young person to be over 16.

Intentional sexual touching of a young person under 13 is an absolute offence. This means there can be no defence in such a case that it was believed the person was over 16. Sexual touching (which involves penetration of the vagina, anus or mouth by the penis or penetration of the vagina or anus with a part of the body or any object) is punishable by up to life imprisonment. Sexual touching not involving penetration is punishable by up to 14 years' imprisonment.

What can you do if you are concerned about your child being sexually abused?

Although you will feel upset yourself, the NSPCC advises you to try not to react in a way that adds to your child's distress by, for example, displaying disbelief or blame. Try your best to:

- keep calm;

- listen very carefully to what your child tells you;

- make clear that you believe what they are telling you;

- allow your child to tell you as much as they want to about the abuse, but do not force them to talk about it;

- tell your child that they have done the right thing in telling you;

- tell them that they are not to blame for the abuse.

Contact the NSPCC Child Protection Helpline immediately (0808 800 5000). The advisers are qualified child protection officers and advise on stopping and reporting the abuse. Alternatively, contact your health visitor, GP, or your local police or social services immediately. Do not confront the abuser yourself. Your priority must be to stop the abuse and protect your child.

The NSPCC defines 'sexual abuse' as when a child or young person is 'pressurised, forced or tricked into taking part in any kind of sexual activity with an adult or young person. This can include kissing, touching the young person's genitals or breasts, intercourse or oral sex. Encouraging a child to look at pornographic magazines, videos or sexual acts is also sexual abuse.' There is advice on the NSPCC website and it also runs ChildLine, a free and confidential, 24-hour helpline for children in distress or danger.

CONTACTS

Staying in

For information on children being left alone, babysitting and disciplining children, see the National Society for the Prevention of Cruelty to Children (www.nspcc.org.uk) as well as the Royal Society for the Prevention of Accidents (www.rospa.com). Information on broadcasting standards is available from Ofcom (www.ofcom.org.uk), and the film and video classification regime is the responsibility of the British Board of Film Classification (www.bbfc.co.uk) and you can also go to www.pbbfc.co.uk, the BBFC's site for parents (where you can also search for individual films and read viewing advice). The Voice of the Listener & Viewer (VLV) represents the citizen and consumer interest in broadcasting and campaigns for quality in British broadcasting. For more information, see www.vlv.org.uk. For information on child protection on the Internet, see the Child Exploitation and Online Protection (CEOP) Centre's website (www.ceop.police.uk).

For information about downloading music online legally or not, see the British Phonographic Industry website (www.bpi.co.uk). Guidelines on the content of magazines aimed at teenagers is available at the Teenage Magazine Arbitration Panel site (www.tmap.org.uk).

Going out

For information about child safety in cars, see www.childcarseats.org.uk

and for information about safety on trips, see Adventure Activities Licensing (www.aala.org.uk). You can also check out the website of the Royal Society for the Prevention of Accidents (www.rospa.com), the Health & Safety Executive (www.hse.gov.uk), and the Child Accident Prevention Trust (www.capt.org.uk).

For information on the age at which young people can drink in pubs, see www.drinkaware.co.uk and to find out about proof-of-age schemes, see www.pass-scheme.org.uk. To find out about the conduct of security at nightclubs, you can visit the Security Industry Authority website (www.the-sia.org.uk). The drinks industry watchdog www.portman-group.org.uk has information about the marketing of alcopops.

Health and sex

For information relating to sexual health for the young, see Brook (www.brook.org.uk). It runs a free and confidential helpline (0808 802 1234). The gay rights group Stonewall's website (www.stonewall.org.uk) has information on the law relating to the age of consent. For information about child abuse, see the NSPCC site (www.nspcc.org.uk). The number for ChildLine, the free and confidential, 24-hour helpline for children, is 0800 1111. For information on pregnancy and abortion, see the British Pregnancy Advisory Service site (www.bpas.org).

CHAPTER 7

Growing up: money, work and leaving home

This chapter continues with the broad theme of the previous chapter looking at issues concerning the parents of young people as they grow up and gain independence. It is divided into the following four sections:

1. **Money:** We start our discussion of finances and the young by looking at pocket money and what – if anything – parents typically give their children. We then look at whether your child can open a bank account or acquire 'debt' through, for example, owning a credit card. This section also considers the significance of children learning to save and whether they will be taught the 'value of money'. This section closes by looking at the ways to save on behalf of your children and, finally, whether your child might be eligible for welfare benefits.

2. **Work:** We begin by looking at the age at which school-age children can work (e.g. by taking a paper round) and the special protections afforded to young people in the workplace. We then look at particular issues affecting young people, such as the payment of a 'minimum wage' for young people and children working as models.

3. **Leaving home:** This section considers at what age young people can live independently of their parents. We also consider the support available for a child and a parent when the child leaves home following a dispute.

4. **When parenting fails:** The last part looks at the situations in which

the state will 'step in' to protect children and young people; in particular, the role of social services, child protection and care proceedings.

Money

How much pocket money should you pay your children?

Obviously, that depends on you. It is a highly personal choice. Clearly, older children have different needs to younger ones. The best advice is to ask around.

According to research published in 2008 by the Halifax, the average amount of pocket money was £6.13 per week. Younger children aged between 8 and 11 received over half the amount, £4.34 per week. Pocket money was not keeping up with inflation – the average was £8.37 in 2005. If children saw 'something expensive', less than one-third (29 per cent) saved, most resorted to asking for it for their Christmas or birthday present (43 per cent) and a smaller proportion (17 per cent) used 'pester power'. More than one-quarter of children did not save any pocket money.

Can your child open a bank account?

There are no hard and fast rules about the age at which young people can open bank accounts but, as a general rule of thumb, banks want the account holder to understand what it means to have an account and be able to sign their name. According to the British Bankers' Association, that age generally starts at 11 years, although practice does vary between banks and building societies. Some banks and building societies offer accounts specially designed for younger children, although these are likely to need some parental involvement; for example, an account opened in the parent's name in trust for the child.

Accounts aimed at 11- to 18-year-olds are essentially savings accounts, although some types of account may allow the account holder to buy goods using a card (see later). In these cases, the daily limit for cash withdrawals or purchases is likely to be low and every transaction would be checked to ensure that funds are in the account to avoid it from going overdrawn. Some banks need the permission of the child's parent before issuing a card on the account.

Everyone, including children, has a tax allowance. Provided you, as the parent, complete an HM Revenue & Customs declaration (known as form R85) and hand it to the bank, it will usually pay interest on the money in the child's account without deducting tax.

Banks need to verify the identity of the young person opening the account (and can be fined if they breach strict regulations designed to track movements of money by terrorist and criminal organisations). If you already have an account with the bank, that's reasonably straightforward but otherwise the bank will need to see some form of identification from the parent and something to link them to the child. It is best to check with the bank what sort of ID. Some banks will require the specific permission of the child's parent before opening an account in the child's name. Otherwise, banks can insist that a new customer produces a driving licence or a passport or a recent utility bill in their own name, which obviously puts young people off.

Can your child have credit?

Young people under the age of 18 years cannot generally enter into legally binding contracts. As a consequence, credit cards (issued by banks and building societies) or store cards (issued by high street shops) will not be issued to anyone under 18 years old.

Extra protections are appropriate because, clearly, credit cards are an easy way to make purchases and run up credit (the holder does not have to pay anything until their bill arrives at the end of the month and they then have to pay at least a minimum amount – any balance is then carried over to the next month attracting interest charges). The distinction here is with debit cards, which are not a form of borrowing because when such a card is used to make a purchase the money is immediately transferred from the holder's bank account. Debit accounts are available to customers aged 16 years and over. There are two types of debit card. Young people are most likely to be offered the Solo or Electron kind, where the balance in your account is checked before each transaction. If you have a Maestro or Visa debit card, your account balance won't necessarily be checked and the payment may still go through. Maestro and Visa debit are more widely accepted by retailers. It is unlikely that your child will get overdrawn with a Solo/Electron card but they can with other types of debit card (a point not often realised).

As far as the availability of credit is concerned, there are some less than scrupulous lenders (albeit legit) who will lend to young people who are not able to prove that they have a good credit history. There are also loan sharks, who are unlicensed lenders and operate illegally and offer to lend you money when nobody else will; their rates will be very high and young people may be forced to get a second loan to pay off the first causing their debts to spiral out of control. The Financial Services Authority points out that unlicensed lenders have their own way of avoiding bad debts and 'will often use threats of violence to ensure repayment ... These debts can be difficult to deal with informally and you should contact your local trading standards office, the police or an advice agency if you are experiencing problems with loan sharks'.

Will your child be taught 'the value of money'?

According to Royal Bank of Scotland/NatWest research published in 2007, the overwhelming majority of people (91 per cent) have never received lessons at school on basic financial management, such as budgeting. However, the government added what it calls 'economic wellbeing and financial capability' to the National Curriculum that year. As a result personal finance issues (such as taxation, personal budgeting, pensions, interest rates, trade and investment) will be taught in Personal, Social and Health Education (PSHE) courses. Ministers say it is likely to be 2011 before PSHE becomes a statutory requirement. 'It is essential that we equip our children with the financial skills they will need as adults and get young people thinking about careers and how to fulfil ambitions,' said Ed Balls, as education minister. 'I want teenagers to start learning early how to make the most of their money.' Teachers have also been asked to use Child Trust Funds (see later) as a way of teaching the value of money in maths classes.

Financial educationalists, such as the ifs School of Finance, have been calling on the government to make a stand-alone qualification in personal finance a statutory part of the curriculum 'putting personal finance on an equal footing with other subjects such as geography and modern foreign languages ... compulsory for schools to offer it but not compulsory for all students to take it'. The ifs School of Finance currently provides the only GCSE equivalent qualifications in the subject as well as AS and A level equivalent qualifications in financial studies. Research by the Financial Services Authority (*UK Benchmark Study*, June 2006) reckons that over two-thirds (69 per cent) of secondary schools in England and Wales believe financial education should be made statutory.

The educational charity Pfeg (formerly the Personal Finance Education Group) receives funding from the Financial Services Authority and has as its mission 'to ensure that all young people leaving school have the confidence, skills and knowledge in financial matters to participate fully in society'.

What are the common ways to save for your child's future?

Many parents want to consider their child's financial future from birth. Typically parents think about the cost of higher education, a first car, or a deposit for their child's first home.

There are several options available, including:

- **Child Trust Fund (CTF) scheme:** It became law in 2005 and now every eligible child born on or after 1 September 2002, receives a £250 voucher to be invested in the scheme by their parents. It is a long-term savings and investment account where your child (but no one else) can withdraw the money when they turn 18 and neither you nor your child will pay tax on it. Certain children will get more than £250; for example, children not eligible for Child Benefit because they are in local authority care or those whose family is entitled to full Child Tax Credit. An additional £1,200 each year can be saved in the account by parents, family or friends. Money cannot be taken out of the fund once it has been put in. Once your child is 18 they will be able to decide how to use the money. Children can start to make decisions about how the money is managed when they are 16. The government will make a further contribution to the fund when your child is seven

– all eligible children will receive a further payment of £250 into their CTF account, with children in lower income families receiving an additional £250. You can choose the type of account you want for your child and at any time you can move the account to a different provider or change the type of account. There are three types of account: savings, equity (accounts that invest in stocks and shares) and stakeholders. Your choice depends on what kind of risk you want. Savings accounts are the most straightforward; equity accounts can offer better returns; whereas stakeholder accounts can invest in shares but are subject to government rules to reduce the risks. For example, the money is moved into safer investments when the child reaches 13. Once a voucher has been issued there is a 12-month window in which you can open an account for your child. If you don't, HM Revenue & Customs will open a stakeholder savings account in your child's name.

Once your child reaches 18 the final value of the investment belongs to them and any decisions as to how the money is spent or invested will be the child's.

- **Child Benefit:** Saving this from birth (in 2009 £20 per week for the eldest child and £13.20 per week for each additional child) could build into a lump sum of around £25,000 by the time your child is 18. You will be able to receive Child Benefit if you're bringing up a child under 16 years; a young person under 19 (under 20 in some cases) who is studying in either full-time education or an approved training programme; or a 16- or 17-year-old who recently left full-time further education or approved training and has registered for work or training with the Careers or Connexions Service or similar.

- **Savings deposit accounts:** You can open an account in your child's name. Each year every child has the same personal tax allowance as an adult (£6,475 in 2009/10). However, if the investment money comes from you and any income earned in total in a year from capital invested by you is over £100, it will all be taxable on you – not just the bit above £100. (£100 per parent if you both contribute).

- **Stocks and shares:** The stock market tends to outperform other savings. You can invest in stocks and shares on behalf of your child. As with savings deposit accounts income, income from these investments will be taxed on you if the child's total income infringes the £100 rule mentioned above. And even if income is taxed on the child, tax credits attached to any income paid out cannot be reclaimed even though the child is a non-taxpayer. Any capital gains, however, will be taxed on the child – though bear in mind that the child will be entitled to the annual Capital Gains Tax (CGT) exemption, which is £10,100 in 2009/10 so no tax may actually be payable. As the shares are in fact the child's, you should transfer them into your child's name when they reach 18 years. You are only controlling the investment on behalf of the child until that time.

- **Friendly Societies:** Many of these bonds issued by Friendly Societies are specially designed for children's savings. These are designed so that regular payments are made to the plan for at least ten years. This could be a good way to save regularly for a 'milestone' age such as 18 or 21.

- **Children's bonus bonds:** Issued by National Savings and Investments, these bonds offer a tax-free low-risk way to save in the child's own name. NS&I is backed by the Treasury (www.nsandi.com). You can start saving with as little as £25 up to a maximum of £3,000 in each bond for each child. They offer guaranteed rates of interest for a fixed term of five years. You can then choose to keep the bond for another five years or until the child's 21st birthday. Your child will take control of the bond (or bonds) when they reach 16 years of age. The bond will end on the child's 21st birthday and the final value paid out. It is then up to the child what is done with the funds.

Bear in mind that if an investment is made in your child's name then, while you will control the funds when they are young, they will take control by the age of 18 at the latest – sometimes as early as 16.

Can your child claim welfare benefits?

Possibly; the benefit system is complicated particularly concerning young people. There are benefits for people who are unemployed or on low incomes:

- **Jobseeker's Allowance:** This is a benefit for people who are unemployed but capable of work. They must show that they are fit for work, available, and actively seeking employment. There are two types: contribution-based Jobseeker's Allowance based on National Insurance contributions and income-based, which is based on financial and home circumstances.

It is normally for people aged 18 years and over but particular categories of vulnerable unemployed 16- and 17-year-olds not in full-time education might be able to receive it for short periods if, for example, they are living away from home and likely to suffer hardship. Claimants must have a Jobseeker's Agreement, which is a commitment by the claimant to take certain steps to find a new job. You can find out more information on the Jobcentre website.

- **Income Support:** This is a benefit for people on a low income to help pay for day-to-day living costs. It is normally for people aged 18 years or over. Those aged 16 or 17 may get Income Support if they:

  (i)   have a child or are pregnant;

  (ii) are sick or disabled; or

  (iii) are in a certain kind of educational training and fall into one of the small number of categories such as being estranged from parents.

  Usually 16- or 17-year-olds who have been in care cannot get Income Support but there are exceptions, such as lone parents or disabled young people.

- **Housing Benefit:** Housing Benefit is for people on low income to help them pay their rent (Council Tax Benefit is also for those on low income to help them pay Council Tax). A young person can claim Housing Benefit but the amount payable to a single person under 25 with no children is restricted. They will usually be entitled only to the average rent in the area for a single room with shared facilities, regardless of their actual circumstances and rent. In England and Wales Council Tax Benefit can be claimed only by people aged 18 years or over.

- **Social Fund:** The Social Fund helps people on low incomes pay for one-off expenses which they would not otherwise be able to afford. The fund is limited and loans are discretionary. There are three types of loan – crisis loans, budgeting loans and community care grants. Young people might be able to claim a crisis loan from the Social Fund in an emergency if they are unable to pay for their immediate needs. They do not have to be receiving any other benefits. Someone receiving Income Support or Jobseeker's Allowance may also be able to get a community care grant to help with expenses so that people can live in the community and families can stay together. Alternatively, they might be eligible for a budgeting loan to help cover certain categories of expense including furniture, clothing and travelling. Crisis loans and budgeting loans must be repaid but are interest free.

- **Child Benefit:** This is a flat-rate weekly benefit paid to a person who is responsible for a child under 16 (or a young person under 20 in full-time education up to A level or equivalent or certain approved training courses).

- **Tax Credits:** Young people aged 16 years or over can claim Tax Credits – although mainly have to be over 25 years old. HM Revenue & Customs explains that if you are responsible for a child or young person you can claim Working Tax Credit if you are aged 16 or over and work at least 16 hours a week. If you don't have children, you can claim Working Tax Credit if:

(i)   you are aged 25 or over and work at least 30 hours a week; or

(ii) you are aged 16 or over and work at least 16 hours a week and you qualify for a disability element of Working Tax Credit.

Working Tax Credit is designed in the main for full-time working adults on a low income; however, it is possible for a young person working 16 hours or more a week on a low income with either a disability or responsibility for a child to qualify. Child Tax Credit is payable to over-16-year-olds who are responsible for a child. Those under 16 years cannot claim in their own right but may be included in their parents' claim.

- **Disability benefits:** There are a number including:

Disability Living Allowance (DLA), which has two components – care and mobility – paid at different rates depending on the nature and extent of the disability. The benefit is designed for people under 65 years whose disability means they need extra care or support getting around. It is not means tested and entitlement to DLA can mean that a person becomes entitled to other benefits such as Income Support and can also have the effect of increasing benefits that are already in payment such as Income Support.

- **Employment and Support Allowance:** From October 2008, Employment and Support Allowance replaced Incapacity Benefit. Employment and Support Allowance offers support and financial help for people who are not working due to a health condition or disability.

- **Carer's Allowance:** This is for people who give regular and substantial care to disabled people in their homes. You can't get it if you are in full-time education with 21 hours or more a week of supervised study or earn more than £95 a week.

Work

Your child wants to work around his school hours to supplement his pocket money by doing a paper round – is he allowed?

It depends. Children under the age of 13 years may not as a general rule be employed (Children and Young Persons Act 1933), although local authorities can grant a licence allowing younger children to take part in performances, sports or modelling (see later).

Children are limited to 'light work', defined as the tasks and working conditions which would not be harmful to their health, safety and development and that does not interfere with their education. Children are explicitly not allowed to work in certain jobs in street trading, betting shops, petrol stations or house-to-house charitable collections.

The working week and school:

- **School Days:** Any child of school age may only work 2 hours a day (one hour may be before school).

- **Sundays:** A child of school age may only work 2 hours on any Sunday and then only between 7am and 7pm.

- **Saturdays and school holidays:** Children aged 13 to 14 years can only work 5 hours a day on a Saturday (maximum 12 hours in any week) and only 5 hours a day in a school holiday (maximum 25 hours in any week). If aged 15 to 16 years, they can only work 8 hours a day on a Saturday (maximum 12 hours in any week) and only 8 hours a day in the school holidays (maximum 35 hours in any week).

Every child must have two consecutive weeks away from work during their school holidays each year.

What special protections do your children have at work?

Hours: There are particular protections for young people at work; for example, to prevent them from working long hours and ensuring they take better rest breaks than their older colleagues. For different rules concerning the minimum wage, see later.

Normally, young people aged 16 or 17 should not work:

- more than eight hours a day;
- more than 40 hours a week; or
- at night (but see below).

However, an employer can ask them to work longer hours if they are needed for what the law calls 'maintaining continuity of service or production' or to respond to a surge in demand. A young person can only work these extra hours if the following conditions are met:

- an adult is not available; and
- any training they are doing is not neglected or adversely affected; and
- they are properly supervised if they work at night.

Once someone is over 18 years, they can agree to opt out of the 48-hour average working weekly limit under the Working Time Directive by signing away their rights but under-18-year-olds cannot do this. Even if they want to work longer hours, they cannot. Not every job is covered by this protection but the list of exempted jobs is small. For example, members of the armed forces are not covered by these rules.

Young workers should get a proper break between starting and stopping work every day and a longer period off every week:

- they should have at least 12 hours of rest in every 24-hour period, and this should be a single 12-hour break;

- they should also get a rest period of at least 48 hours in every seven-day period – again, this should be a single break.

This two-day rest break per week is twice as long as workers over 18 years enjoy. Again, young people cannot choose to give this up.

Meal breaks: Young workers should get an uninterrupted break of 30 minutes if they are working for four and a half hours or more. They should be able to take this away from where they work.

Night work: Normally, young workers should not work at night. For these purposes 'night' generally starts at 10pm and ends at 6am. There are some exceptions. Some young people will still be able to work at night but only as long as the following conditions are met:

- the work is needed 'to maintain continuity of service or production', or to respond to a surge in demand;

- an adult is not available to perform the duties;

- their training is not adversely affected;

- they are properly supervised; and

- they are given compensatory rest.

If all of these conditions apply, then they can work throughout the night if:

- they are working in a hospital or somewhere similar; or

- they are working in connection with cultural, artistic, sporting or advertising activities.

In addition, they can work up until midnight or 4am if they work in certain jobs including agriculture, restaurants and bars, or newspaper deliveries.

What special health and safety requirements are there for young workers?

The law demands that employers must be extra-careful with young workers. Unfortunately, there are many examples of employers exposing young workers to high risks. A recent example was teenager Daniel Dennis, who was killed after falling through a skylight on the roof of a Matalan store in South Wales in his first week of a new job. The owner of the roofing business he worked for admitted manslaughter. Daniel's father had warned the employer that his 17-year-old son had received no safety training and should not work at heights.

Before taking on a young worker employers need to assess the risks to his health and the suitability of the proposed work. They should also take into account his relative lack of experience in the workplace.

The Health and Safety at Work Act 1974 applies to all workers whether in a full-time or part-time capacity, in-house or agency, fixed-term or temporary contract, or working for a big company or small firm, even self-employed in some cases. If the worker has a contract of employment, it's up to his boss to make sure he is not exposed to unnecessary risk.

If a worker is 16 or 17 years old, there are special protections in the Management of Health and Safety at Work Regulations 1999. Employers must take account of:

- lack of experience;

- lack of awareness of risks; and

- lack of maturity.

Young people can't do work which:

- is beyond their physical or psychological capacity;

- involves exposure to toxic substances;

- involves harmful exposure to radiation;

- could cause accidents due to their insufficient attention to safety, lack of experience or lack of training; and

- involves health risks from extreme temperatures, noise or vibration.

Unless:

* it is necessary for their training;

* there is supervision from a competent person; or

* any risk will be reduced to the lowest level that is reasonably practicable.

Also, bear in mind that the age discrimination laws apply equally to both old and young alike. In a 2007 Employment Tribunal case (*Wilkinson v Springwell Engineering Ltd*) an 18-year-old office administrator won her claim for age discrimination after having been told by her employer that they were dismissing her because she was 'too young'. Also the UN Convention on the Rights of the Child (article 32) contains the right to be protected from exploitation in the workplace (see chapter 1).

For more information, see the TUC website (www.worksmart.org.uk) – in particular, the *Young People at Work* guide.

Can your child be paid less than £5 an hour?

Yes; the minimum wage was introduced in 1999 – initially set at £3.60. From October 2009, it is £3.57 per hour for 16- and 17-year-olds; £4.83 if you are aged 18 to 21; and £5.80 for over-21s.

Your daughter wants to work as a child model, does she have to be chaperoned?

Possibly. There are special regulations in force to protect children taking part in a performance because it is a recognised area of risk in terms of both poor working conditions and wider child protection issues.

All children under the statutory school leaving age (after the last Friday in June in the school year in which they reach 16 years) need a licence to perform, even babies. The licensing regime is a sensible measure designed to protect the welfare of children, although the legislative framework itself is complicated. It covers two Acts of Parliament (Children and Young Persons Act 1933 and Children and Young Persons Act 1963) and three sets of Regulations. There are some limited exceptions to the need for a licence but if your child will miss school for rehearsals or performances in general terms they must have a licence.

If your child performs without a licence when they should have one, it is illegal. Furthermore, your child may not be covered by insurance if they are injured as a result of an accident.

If your child is involved in anything to do with the entertainment industry and no one has mentioned a licence, then make contact with the child employment team at your local authority. It is up to the local authority to determine exactly what is 'a performance' for the purposes of issuing a licence but generally it covers stage shows, TV programmes, commercials, films and modelling assignments.

Producers often express concern as to what kind of performance requires a licence and what does not. The law is far from clear on this point.

If your child is involved in any show, amateur or professional, including dance shows, the producer should apply for the licence. If your child is registered with an agent, you need to check that the agent or production company is applying. Even if your child is performing outside of the local authority area, the licence has to be issued by your authority.

All children must be looked after either by their own parent or by a registered chaperone or matron while they are taking part in a performance. You cannot look after another child other than your own (even with parental permission) unless you are a registered matron (this requires clearance from the Criminal Records Bureau as well as training). The law states that the maximum number of children an individual chaperone may supervise is 12 although the local authority might consider it appropriate for smaller groups to be supervised by one matron. The regulations make clear that chaperones must remain with the children all of the time other than when they're on stage or performing.

Your child is to take part in a professional stage production – how often can he rehearse?

There are strict rules about the number of performances and rehearsals a child can take part in every week and how many hours in the day. For example, a child may not take part in a performance or rehearsal for more than five days in any period of seven days.

Plus, rules vary according to whether the performances are stage productions or are recorded for future broadcast such as the film or for television. For example, if your child is involved in a stage production, the performance must start at the earliest 10am and end at the latest 10pm if your child is less than 13 years old. If your child is over 13, then the latest time can be 10.30pm (it can be extended by half an hour but not on more than eight evenings in four consecutive weeks and even then not on more than three evenings in any one week). Your child must not take part in a performance that lasts more than three and a half hours and your child's part must not exceed two and a half hours. Your child must not appear in more than two performances or one performance and one rehearsal in one day. There must be an interval of at least one and a half hours between two performances or rehearsals in the same day.

Leaving home

At what age can a young person leave home without parental permission?

A young person can probably leave home at the age of 16 years without the permission of parents or anyone else with parental responsibility, according to the Children's Legal Centre. Residence orders (see chapter 9) come to an end at 16 years and can only be extended in exceptional circumstances. Wardship proceedings under the Children Act (in other words, to make the child 'a ward of court' effectively transferring all responsibility for the child's life to the court) could be brought by you as parents, but the court is unlikely to force a child home. Where there are serious concerns, any person can apply for an emergency protection order or the police could place them in police protection.

If young people are under 17 years, the local authority could apply for a care order. In reality, the courts are unlikely to order anyone aged 16 or 17 years who leaves home against their parents' wishes to return home unless they appear to be in some kind of danger or unable to look after themselves. A child cannot be said to have been 'abducted' unless under the age of 16 years (Child Abduction Act 1984).

Generally speaking, a young person under the age of 16 years cannot 'live independently' under the law. The reason for this is that a local authority can argue that a child's needs are to be met by a parent unless the parent is unwilling or unable to do so in which case they will be subject to child protection proceedings (see later in this chapter). Only at 16 can a child demonstrate their need to live away from home if home-life has become unbearable. However, under existing homelessness law (see below) in order to be classed as homeless the child would have to be made homeless by the actions of his parent as opposed to their own actions.

If your child leaves home following a dispute, what kind of housing and protection from the state could they expect?

It depends. According to the Children's Society an estimated 86,000 children under the age of 16 years run away from home and care each year. Shockingly, the charity reckons that only 12 per cent of local authorities have any services at all for runaways. In early 2008 the government signed up to plans for a national safety net of safe places to go to and safe people to talk to for such children.

There are only two legal options for children under 16 as to where they live if not at home: first, care of social services under the child protection system if parents are abusing, neglecting or harming children which would lead to a care order and fostering, or ultimately and rarely, adoption; and, secondly, fostering under a private arrangement between parents and other adults (although the parents will still be responsible) – see chapter 2 for more on adoption and fostering.

There are a number of potential accommodation options for young people between 16 and 18 leaving home: local authority housing, if they are homeless (provided they are not intentionally so); a private arrangement staying with friends or family; a private licence to rent a house; and local authority accommodation under welfare provisions if their welfare is seriously prejudiced.

Under-18-year-olds can rent privately although they generally cannot enter a contract under the age of 18. They can be granted a licence, though (as opposed to a lease or tenancy) to live in rented housing. The housing and homelessness charity Shelter points out that many landlords refuse to let to 16- and 17-year-olds. Landlords fear that minors cannot be bound by a contract and so they cannot be held liable for rent or hold a tenancy. 'These beliefs have some basis in law, but neither prevents letting to 16- and 17-year-olds,' Shelter reckons.

A young person on low income can apply to a local council for Housing Benefit; however, the amount of benefit will depend upon circumstances. For those under 25 years, single and without children, Housing Benefit will only pay enough for a single room in a shared house (unless they have been in care).

There are also a number of emergency accommodation options such as hostels, night shelters, women's refuges, as well as bed-and-breakfast hotels and staying with friends or family. Children's charities and the government agree that a bed and breakfast or an adult shelter is an unsuitable place for an under-18-year-old.

A council might have a duty to house a young person as part of its responsibilities for homeless people under the Housing Act 1996. In 2002 the government introduced legislation to expand the categories of homeless people who are considered to have a priority need for assistance under the legislation. Before that, 16- and 17-year-olds would have had to have been considered 'vulnerable' in order to have the requisite priority need. Now most under-18s are automatically regarded as having that priority need on account of their age.

In the case of a 16- or 17-year-old presenting as homeless, a local authority is likely to contact parents. This is to check if the young person is actually homeless and their reasons for leaving home to establish that there has been no collusion and to establish whether they have become homeless intentionally (where their actions intentionally lead to them being homeless the council has no legal requirement to help house them).

What can you do if you are concerned about the welfare of your child who has run away from home after a dispute?

If your child runs away from home, you should immediately inform the police. They will advise you on the approach you can take to recover your child. Young children are very vulnerable and will immediately be at high risk with a massive effort going in to finding them. Older children are still at risk and the police have procedures in place for locating them.

If you are in contact with your child, many local authorities run mediation schemes to help parents and children resolve disputes where a 16- or 17-year-old has been made homeless because of a relationship breakdown at home. Authorities will not insist upon mediation in all cases; for example, where there has been violence or abuse. For more information about mediation, contact the National Mediation helpline.

When parenting fails

What responsibility does a local authority have to 'step in' when they have concerns about a child's welfare?

Local authorities, through their social services departments, are under a duty to safeguard and promote a child's welfare. This means, if social workers are worried about a child's welfare, they can take steps to protect them. This may be by making an assessment of need, providing support and services or, if necessary, emergency court action through care proceedings. The overreaching aim of social services is to keep families together.

It is imperative that as soon as a local authority becomes involved with a family, parents receive legal advice. Details of specialist solicitors practising in childcare law are available from the Law Society. Children in care or needing services from local authorities should also have access to specialist legal help.

In what situations might local authorities become involved in the welfare of a young person?

Social services may become involved with children and young people in a number of ways:

1. **The child protection system:** Concerns about a child can be referred to social services by anyone. Some organisations such as schools have a duty to refer a child and will have child protection policies about when and how to do so. Members of the public can also make referrals and can do so anonymously. If you are worried about a child's safety or welfare, the NSPCC has a helpline and information on its website. If you think a child is in immediate danger, call the police on 999. (For information if you are concerned that your child has been abused, see chapter 6.)

    All referrals must be investigated and may result in either an 'initial assessment', a short outline assessment, or a decision that no action is needed. If the initial assessment results in further concerns, the local authority can then start a more detailed 'core assessment' (although it may start emergency court action also if circumstances dictate – see below). A core assessment is a more thorough assessment to address the best way of helping the child with regard to background, needs and family situation. All those involved with the child, including the child, parents and carers, should be involved in the assessment process.

    Where a local authority has made enquiries and suspects that a child in its area has suffered or is likely to suffer significant harm, a child protection conference may be convened. All professionals (e.g. teachers, GPs, health visitors, police, etc.) involved in the child's life will be invited to the conference as will the child's parents or carers. Children are invited to attend. Parents should see a lawyer or at least have taken legal advice before the meeting. In some areas advocacy services for the child may be available.

    At the child protection conference, a social work report should be available setting out the family background and the role of social services to date. The views of parents and child should be included and the report should be available to the parents before the meeting. The meeting is chaired by an officer who is independent of the case. From information provided at the conference and any written reports, attendees must decide whether the child's name should be placed on the Child Protection (or 'at risk') Register and if so under which of one or more of the following categories:

    • neglect;

- emotional abuse;

- sexual abuse; or

- physical abuse.

If a child's name is registered, social services then prepares a 'child protection plan' setting out the needs of the child and the services which will be available to help the child. The aim of the plan is to address problems so that the child's name can be de-registered at the time of the first review held within three months of the initial conference and then, at least, six monthly, after that.

2. **Child in need:** Under the Children Act 1989, every local authority has a duty to safeguard and promote the welfare of children in its area who are 'in need' in an effort to ensure that the upbringing of children by their family is promoted. Following assessment, if it is felt by the social worker that the child (anyone under the age of 18 years) is 'in need', services such as the following may be available:

   - day care for under-five-year-olds not yet at school;

   - after-school, holiday care or activities for school-age children;

   - advice, guidance and counselling;

   - occupational, social, cultural or recreational activities;

   - home helps;

   - help travelling to and from home to use services provided by the local authority;

   - assistance for the child and family to have a holiday;

   - family centres; and

   - financial help.

3. **Care proceedings:** Care proceedings are the court proceedings started by the local authority which if successful, ultimately result in the local authority acquiring 'parental responsibility' (see chapter 1) for the child. Basically, this means that the local authority is then able to decide, amongst other things, where a child should live and with whom the child has contact. Care proceedings should only be started

as a last resort when the local authority feels all other efforts to address the problems in the family which are impacting on the child have failed.

Sometimes, following alleged injury or abuse, emergency action is taken and this can be through:

- **Police protection powers:** A child can be removed and taken into immediate protection by the police if it is felt they might be suffering from or are at risk of suffering from significant harm. This may occur, for example, if the police are called to an incident of violence involving a child and it is felt not safe for a child to remain at home and there is nowhere else for the child to go.

- **Emergency protection orders:** Short-term orders, lasting for no more than eight days initially (although they may be extended for a further seven days), and which allow the local authority to remove a child. It gives the local authority parental responsibility. It can be applied for on short notice or without notice to parents (which is called 'ex parte'). Parents and carers must seek legal advice immediately.

There are also situations where social services have been involved with a family for some time but it remains the view, following assessment, that the child is at risk of suffering harm. If so, the local authority may then decide to make an application to the court for a 'care order'.

Care proceedings are often long and complicated but ultimately the test for the court on deciding whether to make an order, is whether the child is suffering or is likely to suffer from significant harm.

During the care proceedings, the local authority will gather evidence to support its case including reports from social workers. There may be reports from medical or other experts too depending on the circumstances of the case. Parents can also offer evidence to support their case. Others, such as the extended family, can become involved. For example, a grandparent may want to be considered by the court as possible carer.

Again this is another situation where it is essential that parents and potential carers of the child obtain legal advice. Parents with parental responsibility in care proceedings (see chapter 1) are automatically entitled to legal aid regardless of their financial circumstances. At the start of the care proceedings, the child will be allocated a solicitor. If the child is young and not capable of understanding the proceedings, the child's solicitor will receive instructions from the child's guardian. The guardian, usually a former social worker, works independently of all other parties and their role is to report to the court on the child's wishes and feelings and their view on the best interests of the child. Where a child is older and able to understand the proceedings and the child does not agree with the view of the guardian, the child then instructs their solicitor direct.

When a care order is made, the local authority then gains parental responsibility for the child. This allows the local authority to make decisions about the child's upbringing such as where they will live, which school they will go to, details about contact with their family, etc. All this information is contained in the child's 'care plan'. The parents retain parental responsibility on the making of a care order and should be consulted about decisions concerning the child in care, but the reality is that once a care order is made, the local authority takes over the decision-making and parenting role.

Once a care order is made, the guardian and child's solicitor role ends too. This means that accessing legal advice to challenge a decision of a local authority can be very difficult for a child once they are in care. A child growing up in care may need independent advice about issues like proposed changes of placement, non-allocation of social worker and breakdown in contact. In many areas in the UK, advocacy services are available to young people in care which may be able to assist the young person accessing legal advice. Any child 'looked after' by the local authority (i.e. either a child subject to a care order or a child accommodated under the Children Act, section 20, see below) is entitled to an advocate when making a complaint against a local authority.

The voice of the child in care should also be heard through the independent review process. A review meeting should be held at least every six months. At this meeting, at which the child, parents, social worker and other professionals involved with the child are invited to attend, all aspects of the child's welfare should be considered and the child's views heard. The reviews are chaired by an independent reviewing officer, a local authority employee who is independent of the child's case. In some circumstances, if the independent reviewing officer is concerned about the activity or inactivity of the local authority, the child's case can be referred to the Children and Family Court Advisory Support Service (CAFCASS). CAFCASS was set up in 2001 under the Criminal Justice and Court Services Act as an independent body (independent of the courts, social services, education and health authorities) to 'safeguard and promote the welfare of children' and to provide for children to be represented.

CAFCASS may then refer the case back to the original child's guardian or elsewhere for legal representation. In reality this rarely happens, making it difficult for children in care to access independent advice and representation.

4. **Accommodated children:** Sometimes a parent is unable or unwilling to continue to care for a child. In some cases a local authority has a duty to provide accommodation, usually in the form of a foster placement or children's home. Alternatively, that decision may be at the discretion of the local authority. Often it can be difficult, particularly if the child is over 16 years, to persuade the local authority to 'accommodate' the child.

    If an authority agrees to 'accommodate' a child, that child becomes known as a 'looked after child'. Children subject to a care order are also 'looked after'. The main difference between a child 'looked after' under the Children Act, section 20, and a child who is in care because of a care order, is that the local authority does not share parental responsibility for the child. Where a child is accommodated under the Children Act, the local authority has similar responsibilities as it has towards a child in care. Amongst many other things, there must be reviews by an independent reviewing officer at regular intervals, the child should have a social worker, the child should be consulted about decisions affecting them, and consideration should be given to contact with family.

What if a child is concerned about their care provision?

Every local authority must have a formal written complaints policy. It must also ensure that any child making a complaint about his care provision has the benefit of an advocate to help them. Complaints can also be made by children direct to the Children's Commissioner and the Children's Rights Director. The Local Government Ombudsman is also able to investigate complaints and may direct local authorities to change policies and award compensation. The Ombudsman has a separate procedure to deal with cases referred to it by children.

Alternatively, if a decision has been made by a local authority outside the scope of its powers, this decision may be challenged through the courts by way of judicial review. A judicial review is an examination by the court of an administrative decision to determine whether that decision has been made properly (i.e. it's not about whether the decision was good or bad).

To use this process all other remedies such as complaints procedures should be used first although if the case is an emergency, for example, concerning a child in care being made to move to a placement without any consultation, this will not be possible.

When does a child leave the care system?

Care orders end at the age of 18 years. Generally, the planning for leaving care starts at the age of 16 years. In the past, a major criticism of the care system has been that many 16-year-olds move on with a lack of planning and support. However, recent proposals for change suggest that children in foster placements should be entitled to remain in those placements until after the age of 18 years in line with many children living at home. The local authority has various responsibilities towards children leaving care which differ depending upon the involvement the local authority has had with the child in the past.

Generally, a child leaving care is entitled to a 'personal adviser' and a 'pathway plan', which after assessment just before the child's 16th birthday sets out how the support, accommodation, education and developmental needs of that the young person are best met.

It is generally accepted that in the past support at the time of leaving care has been inadequate and measures are gradually improving to ensure that care leavers have better access to support and advice.

CONTACTS

Money

For information on young people and money, see the Citizens Advice Bureau's advice guide (www.adviceguide.org.uk). The Financial Services Authority has useful guidance on its website relating to young people, credit and debt (www.moneymadeclear.fsa.gov.uk). To find out more about debit and credit cards, see www.moneymadeclear.fsa.gov.uk/products/paying_for_things/plastic_cards.html. There is an online resource for young people about their finances at www.youthmoney.com, written by the journalist PJ White. To find out more about eligibility for welfare benefits, see www.jobcentreplus.gov.uk.

Work

For information on young people and work, see the TUC's workSMART guide (www.worksmart.org.uk). For information about children working in entertainment, see Surrey County Council's (www.surreycc.gov.uk), where you can download a guide to the law.

Leaving home

For more information about homelessness, see Shelter's site (www.shelter.org.uk)and the Children's Society's site (www.childrenssociety.org.uk).

To find out about mediation services, see the National Mediation Helpline (www.nationalmediationhelpline.com). The charity Missing People (formerly the National Missing Persons Helpline) has information and support for parents of children who run away from home (www.missingpeople.org.uk). It also runs the Runaway Helpline, the national, freephone confidential service for anyone who has run away from home or been in care.

When parenting fails

If you are worried about a child's safety or welfare, see the NSPCC website (www.nspcc.org.uk) and there is also a helpline (0808 800 5000). If you think a child is in immediate danger, call the police on 999. ChildLine is the free and confidential helpline for children in distress or danger (0800 1111).

A list of specialist lawyers who are members of the Law Society's Children Panel who deal with care proceedings is available at www.lawsociety.org.uk. Lawyers for Young People at the Children's Society (www.childrenssociety.org.uk/lfyp) is able to provide advice for children and young people in care. For information about children in care and how complaints can also be made by children, see the Children's Commissioner (www.11million.org.uk) and the Children's Rights Director (www.rights4me.org.uk). The Local Government Ombudsman (www.lgo.org.uk) is also able to investigate complaints.

CHAPTER 8

Wrong side of the law

There has long been a debate in the media about the extent to which New Labour's policy on anti-social behaviour has contributed to demonising the young as 'hoodies' and even unnecessarily criminalising many young people. A 2008 report showed that almost 1,000 children aged 10 to 17 had been jailed for breaking anti-social behaviour orders (ASBOs) between 2000, when they were launched, and the end of 2006 (plus another 300 to 400 estimated for 2007/08). Professor Rod Morgan, a former chief inspector of probation and chairman of the Youth Justice Board, argued that an increase in fixed penalty notices and cautions was expanding the number of people with criminal records. 'There is a good deal of anecdotal evidence, for example, that behaviour, particularly that of children and young people, is being criminalised which arguably would be better dealt with informally, and in previous times was,' he said (*Independent*, 25 August 2008). Whatever your view of ASBOs, many parents of teenagers will acknowledge just how easy it is for their children to attract the wrong kind of attention from the police. This chapter considers what happens if your children get into trouble.

First, we look at the age at which young people become responsible under the criminal law for their own actions and how the court system deals with young people. We then consider whether a child has a right to privacy if they come before the court.

We also deal with the common offences committed by the young and how they are dealt with and, in particular, laws focusing on anti-social behaviour.

This chapter then looks at punishment, from a police officer's powers to administer 'a slap on the wrist' to the young to more serious punishment meted out by the courts.

Finally, the chapter deals with parents – whether they can be held responsible under the law for the acts of their children and when they need legal advice.

At what age do young people become responsible under the criminal law for their actions?

Children are generally liable under criminal law for their own actions from the age of 10 years old, although the younger the child, the less likely it might be that the child intended his actions or was acting recklessly. It should also be noted that children under the age of 10 can be arrested for having committed criminal acts, even though they cannot be later charged with having done so. The reason for this apparent quirk in the system is that it allows for intervention by agencies outside of the mainstream criminal justice system, notably social services.

New Labour's focus on anti-social behaviour has meant a greater interest in the more low-level criminal behaviour and nuisance and so it is more important than ever for both children and parents to know the boundaries of acceptable behaviour, which are more tightly drawn than many parents would believe.

There has been pressure on the UK to raise the age of criminal responsibility. For example, in 2005 Alvaro Gil-Robles, the human rights commissioner at the Council of Europe, recommended that the age of criminal responsibility in Britain should be raised to the levels of other European countries, where children generally have limited responsibility from 13 or 14 and full responsibility at 18. In his report, he expressed surprise that the age of criminal responsibility was 10 in England and Wales and just 8 in Scotland. He was reported to have 'extreme difficulty in accepting that a child of 12 or 13 can be criminally culpable for his actions in the same sense as an adult'. In the prosecution of the two 10-year-olds, Jon Venables and Robert Thompson, who killed the toddler Jamie Bulger in 1993, it was argued that they knew that what they were doing was seriously wrong and therefore they were given prison sentences.

How do the courts deal with youngsters?

Children prosecuted for criminal offences will be dealt with either in the Youth Court, a specialist division of the magistrates' court, or at a Crown Court. The venue will very much depend on the seriousness of the alleged offence, with only the more serious incidents warranting Crown Court trial. The idea is that a Youth Court is specially geared to young people and deals with cases in a speedier and more sensitive fashion. One potential disadvantage is that they are denied the right to elect juries in a large number of cases.

How does a Youth Court work?

Proceedings are heard in a courtroom at the local magistrates' court, generally before three magistrates. The proceedings lack the formality and pomp of the Crown Court, but it would be wrong to think of them as being informal. Most magistrates take the view that the dignity of proceedings is essential to ensure that young people appreciate the full seriousness of coming before a court. It is also common in most Youth Courts for the magistrates to actively engage with and challenge the young person in relation to their behaviour. That said, there are no wigs or gowns and it is solicitors rather than barristers that generally conduct all of the cases in that court, including the most serious. Sentencing of those found guilty can range from referral orders (in which the court orders the offender to work closely with a panel of professionals in order to address offending behaviour) through to detention for up to two years.

By contrast, serious crimes such as murder, rape, some robberies and other serious offences will be dealt with before a judge and jury in the Crown Court. The proceedings are altered slightly in order to provide for a less intimidating environment – proceedings will be conducted with wigs removed, court sessions will be shorter and in some cases a less imposing court layout. But the general impact of proceedings in the Crown Court should not be underestimated, nor should the court's powers when it comes to sentence (up to life imprisonment in some cases). While the Crown Court is able to deal more robustly with young defendants, it also works in a much more sympathetic way when the need arises. Lawyers often welcome the idea that young clients end up in the Crown Court as they believe that the judge will be more inclined to take a much more balanced approach.

Does a child have an absolute right to their privacy if they end up in court?

No, in fact, there has been far more reporting of cases involving young defendants in recent years, as the balance has shifted from protecting the rights of the child criminal to 'naming and shaming' in order to inform local communities. This shift has been particularly conspicuous in cases of anti-social behaviour.

A court must conduct a sensitive balancing exercise remembering the following principles: 'In determining whether something is in the public interest, the court must have regard to the open reporting of crime, the open reporting of matters relating to human health or safety and the prevention and exposure of miscarriages of justice as well as to the welfare of the person in relation to whom the restriction would apply and views such a person, or in the case of a person under 16, his parent or other appropriate person, may have expressed' (Judicial Studies Board guidance).

Children and parents must be aware therefore that serious crimes will often now be reported in the media, with the appetite for stories increasing with the seriousness of the crime. It is now only in routine and, ironically, the gravest cases (e.g. the Bulger case) that young persons are protected from media reporting.

What are the common offences committed by the young?

*   **Alcohol:** It is an offence to sell alcohol to those under the age of 18 and those young people found in possession will have it confiscated.

    Drink-driving is the most common drink-related offence and leads to a driving ban for a minimum period of 12 months and in most cases much longer. This can affect a young person's job prospects and will inevitably mean that their first car is far in the future if only because of the prohibitive insurance premiums that will follow. Drink-related crime features very highly in youth court cases.

- **Drugs:** Mixed messages, particularly in relation to the use of cannabis, which has become a great deal stronger in recent years, has led to widespread confusion in relation to drug possession. The Misuse of Drugs Act 1971 regulates what are called 'controlled drugs'. It divides drugs into three classes: class A (including cocaine and crack, ecstasy, heroin, LSD, methamphetamine (crystal meth) and magic mushrooms); class B (including cannabis, amphetamine and barbiturates) and class C (including amphetamines, anabolic steroids and minor tranquillisers).

  It remains a criminal offence to possess any controlled drug, including cannabis and, unlike adults, young persons under 18 years old are not eligible for informal warnings or penalty notices. This means that in most cases they will have their conduct formally marked by a reprimand or final warning.

  For dealing and trafficking class C drugs, the maximum penalty is 14 years rising to life imprisonment for class A drug offences. Possession of even small quantities of class A drugs is treated seriously and may result in detention. Children are often used by drug dealers and even limited involvement with drugs is a serious offence. Drug dealing carries heavy penalties, even where it is not carried out for a profit (e.g. supplying to friends). Most medicines are not controlled drugs but they are nonetheless strictly regulated, and dealing in them is a criminal offence; this includes common substances such as the stimulant ephedrine, widely used by body builders.

  There is a strong link between acquisitive offending and drug use as those addicted steal ever increasing amounts in order to fund their addiction. While there are community orders that can go some way to addressing substance misuse, they should not be considered a light option and will involve a strong commitment from the offender if they are to work.

  For a first offence of cannabis possession young people under 18 years will be arrested, taken to a police station where they will be interviewed under caution, fingerprinted, photographed and have their DNA taken and given a formal warning or reprimand and have an entry against their name on the Police National Computer. Further offences will lead to a final warning or charge.

- **Theft:** Theft (maximum penalty seven years) is the dishonest taking of property and robbery (maximum penalty life imprisonment) is theft with the use or threat of force in order to take property (Theft Act 1968). Thefts range from simple shoplifting through to violent street robberies. Mugging is taken extremely seriously by the courts. Courts are also likely to take a strong line in robberies involving weapons, particularly knives, as these offences often have unintended outcomes – not least when people end up facing murder charges, when all they set out to do was frighten and take a pair of trainers or a mobile phone.

- **Carrying a weapon:** It is an offence for any person to have a knife, blade or other type of offensive weapon on them while in public and especially on school premises (Offensive Weapons Act 1996). A police officer can come on to school premises to search anyone who is believed to be in possession of a weapon and also to arrest them. A person found to be in possession of an offensive weapon may be able to rely on limited defences (e.g. the weapon is used for work or part of a national costume). It is also an offence to sell a knife or a similar type of weapon to a person under 16 years of age. All of these weapons offences under the 1996 Act carry imprisonment and can even go to the Crown Court.

- **Criminal damage:** Criminal damage is the intentional or reckless damaging of property, ranging from smashing windows with stones through to setting fire to warehouses (arson). Many offences result in grave yet unintended consequences (throwing stones at cars leading to motor accidents and setting fire to seemingly unoccupied buildings leading to death), and it is for this reason that young people need to be particularly aware that they will generally be liable for unintended consequences of their behaviour.

- **Anti-social behaviour:** Contrary to popular belief there is no crime of 'anti-social behaviour', and the term is used in law to denote behaviour that causes harassment, alarm or distress to another. Some acts, such as violence, meet that definition in almost all cases; in some instances even things such as criminal damage or littering might be classed as anti-social behaviour. New Labour introduced the anti-social behaviour orders (ASBOs) regime (under the Crime and Disorder Act 1998) to deal with this particular problem and they are civil orders that seek to impose restrictions on what a young person or adult can and cannot do. Breaches of ASBOs are dealt with severely and detention of up to two years can be imposed in the most serious cases. A whole raft of laws were brought in (under the Anti-Social Behaviour Act 2003) to stop low-level anti-social activities (many of which affect young people) including cycling on the pavement, truancy (see chapter 5), hoax 999 calls, letting off fireworks, and drunkenness in public.

Where a young person is behaving in a consistently anti-social manner, each individual act might of itself be at the lowest end of the scale of offending and cumulatively present a problem for either the repeat victim or the wider community.

Cannabis and the law

1970: Designated special class B category halfway between 'hard' and 'soft' drugs, as a compromise between Labour Home Secretary James Callaghan, who believed it was as dangerous as heroin, and a 'student faction' in cabinet who did not.

1978: Advisory council on misuse of drugs recommends downgrading cannabis from class B to class C to put it on a par with tranquillisers. Labour Home Secretary rejects advice.

2002: Advisory council on misuse of drugs looks again at legal status of cannabis at request of the then New Labour Home Secretary David Blunkett, and again recommends downgrading it from B to C, saying it was less harmful than other class B drugs such as amphetamine.

2004: David Blunkett downgrades cannabis. It is still illegal but police adopt a policy of 'confiscate and warn'. Maximum prison sentence for possession cut from five to two years.

2005: Charles Clarke (as Home Secretary) asks the advisory council on the misuse of drugs to review evidence on the effects of strong cannabis on mental health. The council decides to confirm its status as a class C drug but issues a reminder of its harmfulness.

2007: Another New Labour Home Secretary, Jacqui Smith requests further review amid anxiety about more potent strains and impact on mental health.

2009: The government recategorises cannabis as a class B drug, against the advice of the advisory council (a number of the scientists resign from the council).

Are ASBOs criminalising the young?

Youth groups, civil liberties campaigners and concerned parents have all argued that ASBOs have the effect of 'criminalising the young'. ASBOs can be served against children as young as ten years.

The criteria that the magistrate must use in deciding to impose an ASBO is that the individual has behaved in a manner 'that caused or was likely to cause harassment, alarm or distress', and that the order is necessary to stop the behaviour recurring. Breaching the conditions of an order is a criminal offence, punishable by up to five years in prison. The government said that ASBOs would only be imposed on children 'in exceptional circumstances' but (according to the campaign group Asbowatch) more than four in ten orders have been imposed on young people aged less than 17 years old. Many have been imposed on children with special needs. A 2007 study by the British Institute for Brain Injured Children found that up to 35 per cent of young people with ASBOs had a mental disorder or learning difficulty. Anyone who gets an ASBO can be publicly 'named and shamed' – in other words, your photo and personal details can be distributed by leaflets, posters and on the Internet.

What powers do the police have to give the young 'a slap on the wrist'?

There is an increasing tendency to treat young people's brushes with the law out of court wherever possible. Young offenders frequently receive warnings or reprimands in relation to their behaviour – in other words, a dressing down from a senior police officer.

The use of fixed penalty notices for offences ranging from drunkenness to making nuisance calls, previously not used outside of road traffic crimes, is now extremely common. The fines themselves can be hefty (up to £80, at the time of going to press) and the notices also recorded for future reference (however, this does not need an admission of guilt and therefore is not the same as a reprimand or final warning, where both an admission and clear admissible evidence should be present). It is always tempting to take up such an offer as opposed to having to go to court with the upset and inconvenience that carries. It is vital that you consider carefully the wider implications before being tempted to agree, though, as the record of the final warning may appear many years later in relation to searches in a range of situations (e.g. jobs, immigration control) and a person may well ask why a penalty was accepted if you had done nothing wrong. An innocent person should always maintain their innocence.

How are young people punished?

Punishment following conviction depends very much on the nature and circumstances of the crime, along with a consideration of the particular characteristics of your child. The courts recognise that the immaturity of youth tempts some along the wrong path, and that other crimes are born out of moments of stupidity or intoxication. First-time and sometimes second-time offenders before the courts, save for the most serious matters, will receive a referral order. This is a direction to appear before a referral panel, a group of professionals and lay people who will work with you and your child to identify any underlying problems that may have contributed to the offending behaviour and work towards resolving those. A multi-agency approach often means that offending behaviour can be nipped in the bud before it escalates out of control.

Repeat offenders can be sentenced to financial penalties (payable by you, the parents) or community orders of various descriptions. The idea is to mark the offending behaviour with a consequence and in relation to community penalties also to provide a constructive framework for rehabilitating the offender and discouraging future offending behaviour.

At the extreme end, either for the offender committing a serious crime, or for the repeat offender, prison might be the only option. In March 2008 the total number of under-18-year-olds in custody was 2,942. The consequences of offending often outlast the period of punishment, with publicised court appearances harming the child's prospects of settling in a community, and the need in many instances to declare the conviction when applying for jobs. Some convictions (e.g. for violent offences) may prevent your child working with children (e.g. childcare), and others (e.g.

drugs offences) result in entry into foreign countries, notably the USA, being denied. Previous convictions can also be cited in other criminal proceedings in many cases, so the past is not always capable of being easily left behind.

Can parents be liable for the criminal acts of their children?

Parents are not directly liable in criminal law for the actions of their children, but consequences will follow, ranging from having to attend court to accompany the child to hearings right through to paying fines or attending parenting classes. The courts recognise that in the vast majority of cases children offend because proper boundaries have not been set at home.

My child is arrested – do we need legal help?

There are various stages at which you might want to take legal advice from a solicitor. The first stage is on arrest when your child has been taken to the police station. You are likely to be called upon to attend the police station to act as an 'appropriate adult' to support your child. Young people under the age of 17 must have an 'appropriate adult' with them when they are interviewed by the police. That appropriate adult can be a family member, friend or often a volunteer or healthcare professional and there are groups of trained volunteers who can do this as well. This can happen by appointment with a police officer when you and your child attend the police station for a pre-arranged arrest.

There will be a stage when you are asked if you want the services of a lawyer. You can make your own arrangements, where you may have to pay privately for their attendance (if the solicitor does not undertake legal aid work). If the solicitor has a legal aid contract with the Criminal Defence Service, then he may be prepared to advise your child or you can ask for the duty solicitor, who will be assigned to you from a panel of local solicitors who undertake legal aid work.

If you choose not to instruct a solicitor at the police station and your child is charged or summonsed with an offence, you may then wish to instruct a solicitor to represent him. You should make contact with a solicitor as soon as possible who can advise you as to whether legal aid will be available or not. Legal aid is generally granted except for the most trivial offences and there is no assessment of financial means.

The final time when you might come into contact with a solicitor is if you have chosen not to instruct one and arrive at court and decide you would like legal advice or if the court feels that you would benefit from legal advice. In these circumstances, you may be directed to a court duty solicitor. You should note that the court duty solicitor can only advise in limited circumstances and cannot undertake trials or advise on certain 'low-level' offences as these do not fall within the scope of their remit. It is for this reason that if you want your child to be represented early contact with a solicitor after charge or summons is essential.

Are children automatically eligible for legal aid?

Yes, for a criminal matter. Legal aid is automatic and there is no means test. For non-criminal matters, children are not always entitled to legal aid. There are different rules for different services. For general advice and family disputes, if a child applies for legal aid the means of the parent are also taken into account (unless there is a conflict of interest between parent and child). However, for representation in non-family cases (e.g. a clinical negligence claim on behalf of a baby or child injured in hospital) children are assessed on their own means and so are almost certain to be financially eligible. All cases remain subject to merits criteria so that only cases with reasonable prospects of success can be funded. To find out more about legal aid, contact the Legal Services Commission.

CONTACTS

For more information about youth justice, see the Youth Justice Board for England and Wales (www.yjb.gov.uk).

For more information about legal aid, see the Legal Services Commission (www.legalservices.gov.uk).

CHAPTER 9

Living together and living apart

This chapter falls into two parts. The first half considers how families live together – as man and wife, unmarried cohabitants, and civil partners – and the differing degrees of protection those various relationships offer to partners and to children. The second half looks at divorce and breaking up.

- **Living together:** We start by taking a look at why couples should get married from a strictly legal point of view – in other words, what are the protections and rights afforded by choosing the institution of marriage? Increasingly, people in England and Wales are choosing to live together without getting married – in 2007, it was reckoned that there were over four million of us living together as man and wife without being married. Unfortunately, many people wrongly believe that after a couple of years they become 'common law' husband and wife, with the same protections as married couples. We then consider pre-nuptial agreements, who can get married, where and how.

  The second part of this section compares the relative lack of protection afforded to unmarried couples (gay or straight) and their children and the value of making wills.

- **Living apart:** The second half of this chapter considers what happens when couples break up. Since 1971, the overall divorce rate has doubled (and the number of marriages has halved). According to the Office for National Statistics' figures in 2004 more than 4 out of every

10 couples getting married (45 per cent) were likely to end in divorce. However, it appears that the credit crunch might have halted the trend and the most recent figures (published 2009) show the divorce rate in England and Wales dropping for the third year in a row (from 12.2 divorcing people per thousand married people in 2006 to 11.9 in 2007).

We start with a general discussion of what happens on a break-up, what it means to divorce and whether there are alternatives to divorce.

We then consider arrangements for your children if you split with your partner such as residence, contact, financial support and the role of the Child Maintenance and Enforcement Commission (formerly the Child Support Agency (CSA)). Next we look at what happens to the home on a split. We also consider ways in which couples can take the acrimony out of divorce or relationship break-up. Finally, we look at what you can do to protect yourself and your child from a violent partner and how the police handle allegations of domestic violence.

Living together

Is it worth getting married?

Clearly that's a difficult question and requires a consideration of subjective issues. People get married for many different reasons. Many couples want to celebrate the 'big day' whereas others take a more pragmatic view wanting to 'formalise' their relationship. Those couples who choose not to marry also do so for a variety of reasons. Some have been through unsuccessful marriages previously and don't want to do it again others approve of the institution of marriage, yet simply never get round to tying the knot. Some want to preserve their independence within a relationship – that is not always clear or welcome to their partners.

From a strictly legal point of view, there are considerable protections provided by law for married couples that unmarried couples don't have. Increasingly, more and more people are choosing not to marry. Couples living in 'unmarried bliss' should be aware that they have few rights compared to married couples (or civil partners). Unfortunately, the 'myth of common law marriage' (the mistaken notion that partners acquire the same rights as married couples over the years) has proved remarkably persistent. This is so despite the fact that common law marriage hasn't existed in England and Wales since 1753. Worryingly, recent research shows that almost two-thirds of us believe that couples who have lived together for a while have the same rights as married couples.

Is a 'pre-nup' likely to be legally binding?

Pre-nuptial agreements ('pre-nup') have an uncertain status in English law. On occasion, the English courts have disregarded them although lawyers report that they are being relied upon. The legal position seems more favourable in Scotland, where a pre-nup has yet to be overturned.

There are a number of obvious issues about contemplating such an agreement. Obviously a pre-marriage contract isn't the most romantic way to begin your relationship. However, it can serve as a pretty effective way of concentrating your minds and determining what you both want out of a relationship (which might not necessarily be the same thing).

In 2008 the viability of the pre-nup in England and Wales received a boost when Susan Sangster, reckoned to be £18 million richer after three previous divorces and described in the press as a serial divorcee, gave up her claim to the fortune of property developer Stuart Crossley. They both signed a pre-nup, but the former model argued that it was invalid as Crossley allegedly failed to disclose 'tens of millions in offshore accounts'. The Court of Appeal upheld the agreement. If ever there was 'a paradigm case', noted Lord Justice Thorpe, for the pre-nup as 'not simply one of the peripheral factors but a factor of magnetic importance' then this was it.

If you want to make a pre-nup watertight, you both need to make sure there has been full and frank disclosure about your respective finances and there is no evidence of pressure from one person on the other to sign the document. Both of you ought to consider independent legal advice and the agreement should be made at least 21 days before the wedding to show that neither party was rushed or forced into the commitment. As time passes, the agreement is likely to be less effective and so you should review it periodically or upon a change in circumstances such as the birth of a child, illness, disability or unemployment. The agreements most likely to be enforceable relate to short-lived marriages where circumstances have remained the same.

Who can get married?

If you are single (whether previously married, divorced, widowed or in a civil partnership that has been dissolved), you can marry anyone except:

- someone already married or in a civil partnership; or

- someone you are not allowed by law to have sex with because of age (they must be over 16 years old), or relationship (such as grandparents, parents, brothers, sisters, children or grandchildren); or

- other relatives (uncles, aunts, nephews or nieces; stepchildren and step-parents; your ex-mother-in-law or ex-father-in-law, etc.).

How old does your child have to be before they can get married?

Again you have to be over 16 years old and if you are under the age of 18 you need the consent of a parent or person with parental responsibility (see chapter 1) or the leave of the court.

Where can they get married?

A marriage can take place in England and Wales at a register office, or a building approved for civil marriage, in an Anglican church or in any other religious building that is registered for marriage ceremonies. The General Register Office website has details.

- **A religious wedding:** Speak to your vicar or see the person in charge of marriages. The church must normally be in the registration district in which you, or your partner, live. People of all denominations have a right to be married in their parish church so if you are Church of England and your partner is a Catholic, it doesn't matter.

If you want to marry in a different church and you are a regular worshipper, then it is usually possible. Otherwise, you would normally be expected to attend services for some time before becoming eligible to be married there. The Church of England in 2007 voted to relax the laws on where couples can get married, giving them new rights to marry in a parish where they have a link. An engaged couple has to demonstrate one of seven 'connections' (such as if you were baptised at the church, confirmed there or previously lived in the area or regularly attended the church). More details are on the Church of England website.

- **A civil marriage:** A civil marriage ceremony can take place in any register office in England or Wales, or at any venue that has been approved to hold a civil marriage (such as stately homes, hotels or restaurants).

What do you have to do to get married?

There are a number of requirements you have to satisfy before you can get married (again, the General Register Office has more details), such as:

- **Residency:** You can get married in England and Wales as long as you have both lived in the area for at least seven days before giving notice of marriage. This applies to all couples, including those travelling from overseas to marry in England and Wales. There are some exceptions.

- **Documentation:** You need to show evidence of name, age and nationality (ideally in the form of your passport). You will also be asked to provide evidence of your address and evidence of the ending of any previous marriage.

- **Notice:** It is a legal requirement to give notice of marriage and, once given, your notice of marriage is displayed on the noticeboard at the register office for a period of 15 clear days. The notice is valid for 12 months and is a legal document required by the Marriage Act 1949 giving the couple's name and surname, age, address, occupation, nationality and marriage venue.

What can unmarried cohabitants do to protect themselves?

There are a number of common sense steps you can take if you don't want to get married but want an approximation of its protections. The importance of at least considering such steps increases significantly if you have or plan to have children.

Some issues you might consider are:

- If you are renting a new place together, think about putting both names on the tenancy (see later).

- If you are buying property, then think carefully about how you might want to own your home. You can own it either as 'joint tenants' or as 'tenants in common'. If you buy as joint tenants, then you own the house 50/50 and the share owned by your partner would pass automatically to you on their death. If you own your home as tenants in common, you can leave a precise share to whoever you choose – you state exactly the nature you share in a declaration of trust. (If you do that, you should make sure you both make a will at the same time, otherwise one of you might end up homeless if the other dies.)

- If you are moving in with your partner and they own the property, you need to discuss how contributions will be made. For example, you need to address the issue of how that contribution might be reflected if you start paying the mortgage or for home improvements. Some people regard their contributions as rent and some homeowners are happy to go further and give their partner a share in the home. The correct paperwork should be put in place. If you have agreed to give your partner a share, it would be best to draw up a declaration of trust. If you have agreed that you (as non-owner) won't have a share, or your contributions will be paid back on break-up, then you can record this in an agreement, called a cohabitation agreement (see later).

- Make a will. Without a will all your personal belongings (and the right to organise your affairs) will automatically pass to the nearest relations that the law recognises (see later). If you haven't finished your divorce, then the nearest relation is, in fact, your estranged husband or wife.

- Sort out parental responsibility of children (see chapter 1).

- Check your pension. Some do not pay survivor's benefits to unmarried partners. Think about how you can build a separate provision for each party.

- Consider a cohabitation agreement (sometimes called a 'living together agreement'). These are likely to be taken into account by the court (and therefore mean you avoid going to court because there is no point). The main reason why they wouldn't be is if you or your partner lied when making them, or if you clearly departed from the agreement at a later date; for example, if you agreed you would never make contributions to the mortgage and then have clearly been paying the mortgage for the last few years. A template agreement is free from the Advice Now website.

You aren't married – what happens if ...

... you move in to your boyfriend's house, have a baby together, and then split up ...?

- Your ex doesn't have to pay you maintenance for your own benefit, even if you've given up work to look after the children or your home, but will still have to pay child support.

- If you rent and the tenancy is in your ex's name only, you will have no automatic right to stay if your ex asks you to leave or walks out (but see later section 'What happens to your home on a split?'). If your ex owns the home (and there's no other agreement), you will have no automatic right to stay if your ex asks you to go but may be able to stay as this is the child's home.

- If there's no other agreement in place, your ex will walk away with all the savings and possessions he built up. If you bought things together but each contributed different amounts to the price, you own the things in the shares in which you contributed.

- If the birth certificate was registered after 1 December 2003, then provided his name is on the birth certificate, he has parental responsibility.

... your partner died suddenly after you had been together for years, but hadn't left a will ...

- You won't automatically inherit anything, including the family home if it's not in your name or your partner's share of the home if you own it jointly as 'tenants in common'.

- You will not get any state bereavement benefit or a state pension based on a percentage of your ex's National Insurance Contributions (which could be a big problem if you have given up work to look after the family).

- If what you inherit is worth more than £325,000 (as of April 2009), you will have to pay Inheritance Tax.

Is it worth making a will?

Yes. For unmarried couples, wills are doubly important. It is estimated that two-thirds of people never get round to making a will. Put starkly: if you aren't married to your partner (or aren't in a civil partnership – see later) and die before you make a will, your partner won't automatically inherit anything from you. By law, it is irrelevant how long you have been together or how much you love your other half. Everything will go to the nearest blood relative.

Not only that, but there are other good reasons to make a will:

- You can appoint a guardian for your children to look after them if you and anyone else with parental responsibility die, and ensure they will be provided for (see below).

- You can select the person to sort out your affairs after your death, otherwise it is the nearest relative.

- You can state your wishes for your funeral.

- You can leave a particular type of tenancy to protect loved ones from having to find a new home after your death.

- You might not have much in life but your estate could receive a compensation or death in service payout, which, without a will, would go to a blood relative and not your partner.

What happens if your partner dies without leaving a will?

Property will be shared out according to the rules of 'intestacy' (if someone dies without a will they die 'intestate'). Only people who are married, civil partners or some close relatives can inherit under those rules. Similarly, if you make a will but it is not legally valid, the rules of intestacy might apply.

You don't inherit anything under the intestacy rules if you are divorced or your civil partnership is dissolved. If you are married or a civil partner at the time of the death of your partner, you inherit under the intestacy rules. If your partner has surviving children, grandchildren or great-grandchildren and the estate is valued at more than £250,000, you will inherit:

- all the personal property and belongings of your partner; plus

- the first £250,000 of the estate; and

- a life interest in half of the remaining estate. This means that if you are entitled to the life interest, you cannot get rid of it or spend that part of the estate. You can, however, have the benefit of it during your lifetime.

As to what happens to your home, it depends on how it is owned. There are two different ways of jointly owning a home: joint tenancies and tenancies in common (see section 'What can unmarried cohabitants do to protect themselves?'). If you and your partner were joint tenants at the time of the death, you will automatically inherit their share of the property. However, if you are tenants in common, you don't automatically inherit their share.

If you have a joint bank or building society account, you automatically inherit the whole of the money. Property and money that you inherit does not count as part of the estate of the person who has died when it is being valued for the intestacy rules.

How do the intestacy rules operate in relation to your children on the death of your partner?

Children of the intestate person inherit if there is no surviving married or civil partner. As stated previously, if you are a surviving partner, then the children will inherit only if the estate is valued at over £250,000. If there are two or more children, the children will inherit in equal shares:

- one half of the value of the estate above £250,000; and

- the other half of the value of the estate above £250,000 when the surviving partner dies.

All the children of the parent who has died intestate inherit equally from the estate. This also applies where a parent has children from different relationships. A child whose parents are not married or have not registered a civil partnership can inherit from the estate of a parent who dies intestate. These children can also inherit from grandparents or great-grandparents who have died intestate. Adopted children (including step-children who have been adopted) have rights to inherit under the rules of intestacy. But otherwise you have to be a biological child to inherit.

Children under 18 do not receive their inheritance immediately. It is managed by trustees on the child's behalf until they reach the age of 18.

If there is no surviving partner, the children of a person who has died intestate inherits the whole estate. This applies however much the estate is worth. If there are two or more children, the estate will be divided equally between them.

A grandchild or great-grandchild cannot inherit from the estate of an intestate person unless their parent or grandparent has died before the intestate person. The grandchildren and great-grandchildren will inherit equal shares of the share to which their parent or grandparent would have been entitled.

Parents, brothers and sisters, and nieces and nephews of the intestate person may inherit under the rules of intestacy. This will depend on several circumstances:

- whether there is a surviving married or civil partner;

- whether there are children, grandchildren or great-grandchildren;

- in the case of nephews and nieces, whether the parent directly related to the person who has died is also dead; and

- the amount of the estate.

Other relatives may have a right to inherit if the person who died intestate had no surviving married partner or civil partner, children, grandchildren, great-grandchildren, parents, brothers, sisters, nephews or nieces. The order of priority amongst other relatives is as follows:

- grandparents;

- uncles and aunts;

- cousins.

Who cannot inherit where someone dies without leaving a will?

Unmarried partners, lesbian or gay partners not in a civil partnership, relations by marriage, close friends and carers. However, even if you can't inherit under the rules of intestacy, you may be able to apply to court for reasonable financial provision from the estate. For example, if you were living with the person who has died, you would not inherit under the rules of intestacy. However, you could apply to court for financial help. You must have lived with them for at least two years. If you were always treated by the person who died as a child of the family, you could apply to the court for help.

What happens if there are no surviving relatives?

The estate passes to the Crown (known as *bona vacantia*). The Treasury Solicitor is then responsible for dealing with the estate. The Crown can make grants from the estate but does not have to agree to them. If you are not a surviving relative, but you believe you have a good reason to apply for a grant, you will need legal advice.

Why appoint a guardian?

As a parent, you need to consider the difficult question of who might take care of your children in the event of your death. A guardian is someone who is appointed to assume responsibility in the event of the death of the child's parent. The appointment is not only appropriate if a child has property or wealth but also covers day-to-day care.

The person who you have chosen will assume parental responsibility provided the appointment is effective (see below). The guardian will have the right to decide on the child's upbringing, healthcare, religion and education.

Who may appoint a guardian?

The Children Act 1989 provides that guardians may be appointed by a parent with parental responsibility for the child (see chapter 1), an existing guardian or by a court order (see later this chapter).

If, on the death of the person making the appointment (even if the parents are separated or divorced):

• there is a surviving parent with parental responsibility; and

• the deceased did not have a residence order in his favour;

then the appointment does not take effect until the death of the surviving parent with parental responsibility. It is then possible that effective appointments by both parents will take effect simultaneously (potentially leading to conflicts between two separately appointed guardians which the court may have to resolve).

Can you refuse to act as guardian?

Yes; even if you are appointed a guardian in someone's will, you can refuse. Such a refusal has to be in writing signed by the proposed guardian and made within a reasonable time of their first knowledge that the appointment had taken effect.

What legal protections do gay and lesbian parents have?

The Civil Partnership Act came into effect at the end of 2005. The landmark legislation enables gay and lesbian couples (aged 16 years and over) to register their relationships. They then have legal status as 'civil partners' meaning that they have rights and responsibilities in much the same way that married couples do. To all intents and purposes, civil partnership is civil marriage with almost the same legal rights.

Figures from the Office for National Statistics released in 2009 showed that 7,169 civil partnerships were formed in 2008, slightly down from 8,728 in 2007, and considerably less than the 18,000 gay relationships in the first year when many long-standing couples were quick off the mark to formalise their relationship.

There is particular relevance here for gay and lesbian parents. If you register your partnership, you become responsible for the other's children and, for example, you will have a duty to provide reasonable maintenance for your partner and any children of the family (provided you treat the children as your own).

More generally, just like marriage, civil partners inherit from each other even without wills and have the right to benefit from each other's National Insurance Contributions plus rights to survivor pensions. They are also exempt from Inheritance Tax on anything that passes between them.

The rights of gay and lesbian couples who don't want to register their civil partnership are much the same as heterosexual couples who don't want to get married.

Living apart

What happens in law when couples break up?

The legal process of a split depends on whether you are married or in a civil partnership or not. If you aren't married or in a civil partnership, then clearly there is no legal process to go through to 'officially' end your relationship. If you are married, then there is, of course, divorce (as well as a number of other less common ways to end your relationship, see later) or 'dissolution' for a civil partnership. It has been reported that there were just 180 civil partnership dissolutions in 2008.

For couples contemplating life apart there are several major issues that need to be considered whether you are married or not:

- **Children:** Where will they live? How will they keep in touch with you and your ex?

- **Your home:** Do you own or rent? Who will pay the rent or mortgage? Will you have to sell or move out?

- **Finances:** Do you have joint or separate accounts? How will you split savings accounts? What about joint debts? What about benefit entitlements? What about pensions and life insurance policies?

- **Wills:** Do you need to change the terms of your will (if, for example, you planned to leave all your possessions to your former partner)?

What does it mean to get 'divorced'?

Divorce is the legal ending of a marriage granted by the courts because there has been an 'irretrievable breakdown' of the marriage. The process is governed largely by the Matrimonial Causes Act 1973 (see below). Before a court grants a divorce, it has to be shown that the marriage has broken down permanently. You do that by completing a legal form called 'a petition' – hence you are the 'petitioner' if you start the divorce and your ex becomes the 'respondent'.

You prove irretrievable breakdown in the petition by establishing one or more of the following five 'facts':

1. **Adultery:** You must prove that your partner has had sex with another person of the opposite sex and that you find it intolerable to live with them. Adultery is defined as voluntary sexual intercourse. That other person can be named in the petition as a co-respondent; however, it is good practice not to as it adds to the acrimony. Not more than six months must have passed since you became aware of the last act of adultery before the petition is sent to the court unless the adultery is continuing. Proof of adultery is rarely needed – often it is admitted.

2. **Unreasonable behaviour:** This is the most commonly cited fact. You have to show that your spouse has behaved in such a way that you cannot reasonably be expected to live with them. Allegations might, for example, include references to excessive drinking or financial extravagance but the court does not insist on severe allegations of

unreasonable behaviour in order to grant a divorce. Relatively mild allegations such as having a lack of common pursuits, spending too much time on the golf course, or at work, are enough. If this sounds an unnecessarily upsetting way of going about things, there is nothing to stop you sitting down with your ex and agreeing what you are going to write.

3. **Desertion:** This is where your spouse has deserted without consent for at least two years. It is almost never cited as it requires the intention to divorce throughout that time.

4. **Two-year separation:** You and your ex have been living apart for at least two years, immediately preceding the presentation of the petition and you both agree to a divorce.

5. **Five-year separation:** You and your ex have been living apart for at least five years immediately before the presentation of the petition. The other spouse need not consent to the divorce.

Couples are often surprised to learn that 'adultery' and 'unreasonable behaviour' are the two reasons cited in most break-ups. The reason for this is because couples generally do not want to have to wait a couple of years before satisfying the other grounds. The law does not allow for divorces in the first year of marriage. In an attempt to take some of the emotional sting out of divorce, a system of 'no-fault divorce' was proposed some years ago (in the Family Law Act 1996). It would have effectively abolished the need to prove adultery or unreasonable behaviour. However, the legislation was never introduced into law. The measures proved too controversial. Many politicians and social commentators regarded the proposals as undermining the value of marriage.

This chapter goes on to consider issues that pertain most directly to parents and children on divorce, but there is a huge amount to consider and it is important you take the proper professional advice. Other issues to consider include the following:

* **Where?** Different countries have very different approaches and so, for example, treat assets on a split very differently. If you or your ex are from another country (or lives abroad), you might want to consider where you divorce. A European law (known as Brussels II) has removed the priority given to English and Welsh law over European

divorce cases in which one person is English or Welsh and the other is from another European country. The court in whichever country in the European Union receives the first petition must take precedence over the court in other countries.

- **Tax?** Separation may create a liability to Capital Gains Tax (CGT), a tax on the increase in value of an asset which becomes payable in the year following disposal of the asset. Any gains on the principal private residence are exempt, and any transfer of the former matrimonial home may not attract CGT provided the owner or owners (whether it was in one party's sole name or held jointly) lived there throughout the period of ownership.

- **Immigration status?** If you are not a British citizen, or have the indefinite leave to remain, consider the impact starting divorce proceedings might have on your immigration status.

- **Loss of widow's status for pensions and trusts on divorce?** As you will never have the chance to become each other's widow or widower, there will be a significant loss of pension benefits to be considered.

What happens on a divorce?

The following short section provides an overview of the legal process. If you are divorcing your spouse, you need to send a divorce petition, court fees, a copy of your marriage certificate, plus a document called 'a statement of arrangements' for the children (see later) to the court. You will then receive a notice of issue of petition from the court to confirm receipt of your petition and to say that a copy of it has been sent to the respondent.

Your ex could defend the divorce by responding within 28 days of receiving the petition. It is unusual, but it could be done for tactical reasons while costs or another issue is sorted.

An undefended divorce is dealt with in the divorce county court or the Principal Registry in London. It is hard to think of any circumstances in which defending a divorce is going to be worth the pain and costs, not least because the eventual hearing will be in public.

If you and your ex agree to break up, then the court will grant what is known as a 'decree nisi', after having considered the petition. The court will have to be satisfied as to arrangements concerning children. After a further period of six weeks following the decree nisi, the petitioner can apply for a court order known as a 'decree absolute', legal confirmation of the split. No court hearing is needed. If there are children, the court will have to satisfy itself that proper arrangements have been made and may want to meet them if they are old enough. You are now free to marry again or enter into a civil partnership.

You can download all the relevant forms from the court service website.

Are there any alternatives to divorce?

Yes; there are a couple, not often used, but nonetheless you might want to consider:

- **Judicial separation:** This is not a divorce and you remain married to your partner. You cannot remarry. It is a halfway house whereby the courts recognise that you and your partner are living apart; however, it is a more formal split than a separation agreement – see below. In terms of the legal process it is similar to divorce. It can be granted for any of the grounds that justify a divorce but it is not obligatory to demonstrate that the marriage has broken down irretrievably. Judicial separation means that the marriage survives, which might be appropriate if, for example, you are opposed to divorce on religious grounds or you want to retain rights under a pension policy. Also the court has powers to resolve issues to do with money or children (which it would not in the case of an informal separation). Only a very small number of judicial separations happen every year compared to divorces.

- **Informal separation:** As a married couple you don't have to divorce. Instead, you and your partner can make whatever arrangements you need (concerning home, maintenance and children) without going to court. You can formalise your own arrangements and draw up your own separation agreement. If you do that, it can be a good idea to take legal advice. This can pose a number of risks including lack of certainty as opposed to the finality of divorce.

You want a 'quickie' divorce. How quickly can you get divorced?

The press often talks about 'quickie' divorces. Speed and the courts are two concepts that rarely go hand in hand and breaking up is no exception. If you want a quick divorce, most legal experts acknowledge that the briefest period is going to be three months as six weeks must elapse between the pronouncement of the decree nisi in court and the decree absolute. That period can be shortened only in extreme circumstances. An application will have to be made and the judge will have to be convinced that there are very good reasons (such as when an ill husband or wife faces imminent death and wants to die divorced). With the delays that exist in most courts, it is usual for the process to take over 20 weeks.

How will you and your ex decide who looks after the children if you can't agree?

When you begin divorce proceedings you must fill out the 'statement of arrangements' form setting out the proposed arrangements for your children. The courts want to know, for example, where the children live, with whom, how often the other parent sees them, where they go to school, and what financial support they receive. In practice, unless you are setting out slightly unusual arrangements, or there is anything else to alert the court, it is unlikely to intervene unless either side makes a specific application.

If it looks as though there is going to be disagreement over arrangements to do with your children, then you can make an application to the court to make certain orders – for example, by ordering contact to take place or to settle specific issues or prohibit certain steps from being taken. These are known as 'section 8 orders'.

There are different types of 'section 8 orders':

- **Residence orders:** These cover where the child should live. The granting of a residence order to someone automatically gives that person parental responsibility for the child if they do not already have it (see chapter 1). Such an order lasts until the child is 16 unless the circumstances of the case are exceptional and the court has ordered that it continue for longer. Shared residence orders are increasingly common providing for children to spend time with both parents.

- **Contact orders:** These detail arrangements for a child to see or have contact with one parent or significant other. Contact orders continue until the child is 16 years. The court will only make contact orders for children over 16 years old in exceptional circumstances. Contact can either be direct (face to face) or indirect (by letter, video, exchange of Christmas cards, etc.). Some orders will be very specific as to times, dates and arrangements whereas others will be left open with the arrangements to be made between the parties. These orders can be for contact between siblings or the child and wider family members and not just for parents. Sometimes orders will give directions that the contact is to be supervised by a third person.

- **Prohibited steps orders:** These are effectively a ban on a child's parents, or any other named person, from taking certain steps that parents would ordinarily take, such as taking a child abroad.

- **Specific issue orders:** These cover how a particular matter should be handled – for example, where a child is to go to school.

Either parent can make an application for such an order whether you are married or not and, if you are married, before you have started divorce proceedings or not. The courts are only concerned about the welfare of the young – under 16 years or between 16 and 18 and still at college or school full time. This includes adopted children, stepchildren or those who have been treated as part of the family but not foster children.

Both the Court Service and CAFCASS (the Children and Family Court Advisory Support Service) have information on applying for section 8 orders on their websites. The court will only make any of these orders if it accepts that making an order is better than not intervening at all. The intention of the law is to free parents up to make decisions for themselves rather than intervene unnecessarily.

Court proceedings concerning section 8 orders generally begin with a conciliation appointment or a first hearing. This will take place in chambers – in other words, in a judge's room and in private. There will often be a CAFCASS officer present known as a children and family reporter. CAFCASS is present to safeguard and promote the welfare of children involved in family court proceedings (see chapter 7).

You may sometimes be asked to talk with the CAFCASS officer in private and without your lawyer to ascertain the issues and try to reach an agreement. It is good advice to always consider mediation (see later) unless that is not going to be possible.

If an agreement can be reached, then the judge will take a view, having consulted with you and your partners' lawyers, as to whether he needs to make an order or simply to record formally the arrangements that have been made.

However, if there is still no agreement, the CAFCASS officer can then advise the court on options. This could be more time with a mediator or CAFCASS officer to assist them to reach an agreement; adjourning the hearing so that they can write what is known as a welfare report on all the children's circumstances; making further enquiries; or proceeding to a court hearing to decide what orders, if any, should be made.

If no agreement is reached, the CAFCASS officer might be asked to write the welfare report giving a view as to what should happen. This takes at least ten weeks and often much longer. The CAFCASS officer is independent of the courts and social services (as well as separate from education, health authorities and other agencies). The welfare of children is their primary concern and they are qualified in social work and experienced in working with children and families. Sometimes agreement can be reached after the CAFCASS report without any need for a final hearing.

The reporter will generally speak with you, your partner and, in particular, your child. If a child is clearly too young (e.g. two years old) then the child will not be directly involved. A joint meeting might be proposed (i.e. with your partner) but you have the right to be seen by yourself especially if you are uncomfortable being in the same room as your partner.

Your child should not be asked to take sides or which parent they like best. According to CAFCASS, 'the children and family reporter will talk with your children about how they can best stay close to both parents – practical things like school and who does what in the family'. The reporter might talk to other people, such as doctors, teachers, relatives, health visitors and social workers. Such enquiries are confidential unless any information is given that a child is at risk.

When the report is finished, it goes to the court, and a copy is sent to your solicitor if you have one or directly to you if you don't. The reporter will let you know who they are talking to and will ask for your agreement when they need to. It is also usual to approach police and social services, including the Child Protection Register.

The court (under the Children Act 1989) has to have the child's welfare as its 'paramount consideration'. The court when considering questions relating to the upbringing of the child must have regard to what is known as 'the welfare checklist' set out in the Children Act 1989, section 1. So the court must consider (amongst other things):

- the ascertainable wishes and feelings of the child concerned (considered in light of their age and understanding);

- their physical, emotional and/or educational needs;

- the likely effect of any change in his circumstances;

- their age, sex, background and any characteristics which the court considers relevant;

- any harm which they have suffered or are at risk of suffering;

- the ability of each of his parents (and any other person in relation to whom the court considers the question to be relevant) to meet the child's needs; and

- the range of powers available to the court under the Children Act 1989 in the proceedings in question.

Although the 'week on/week off' shared parenting arrangements found in the USA are mostly not favoured here, the courts often expect a generous level of contact for a child of school years. It is accepted that it is often best for a child to be mainly at one home during the school week. However, many courts will agree contact arrangements (if geographically close) of alternate weekends collection from school on Friday afternoon and return on Monday mornings and perhaps every Wednesday from school and return to school on Thursday morning. If a father cannot commit to this, the court may give the mother greater financial provision as it is clear that she is taking the greater childcare burden. Similarly courts expect the parents to share half of all school holidays (subject to the age of the child) and alternate Christmases and Easters and other faith days.

Do mothers always get custody?

No, but many fathers believe that they are going to be at a disadvantage when it comes to how courts award residence orders. Family law experts more often than not insist that there is no 'anti-Dad' bias in our legal system. Parents start off on an equal footing. A court will do everything it can to make a decision in the child's 'best interests' (it is required to do so under the Children Act 1989). In other words, a court will take into account all the circumstances, including the feelings of the child and whether they are old enough to understand what is going on.

The court does often find that a baby or a young child will be more appropriately cared for primarily by its mother. However, many fathers are equally capable of caring for their children from an early age and some mothers do not provide the better care. As children grow older, the balance in the mother's favour becomes less pronounced. It might also be relevant that a mother might be available for full-time care.

What happens in the event of a family break-up if you want to keep contact with your grandchildren?

A sad but not uncommon problem arises when parents get divorced and typically the child goes to live with the mother and contact with the child's paternal grandparents is denied. Problems also arise if the parents separate, one dies, or there is a family feud and the grandparents and parents fall out. Again there can be major contact problems when a local authority removes the child from the family and the grandparents want to bring up or at least have regular contact with the children.

If that is the situation, you as a grandparent might consider the following possible remedies:

- **Going to court for a residence or contact order:** These orders can be sought in two different ways. If legal proceedings involving the child have been started by someone else, then grandparents can seek to become involved and ask for such orders to be made. If, for example, the mother and the father have started divorce proceedings, then you can seek to join in those proceedings. Grandparents may also seek to become involved in adoption proceedings or care proceedings.

Grandparents do not have to wait for other proceedings; they can begin proceedings themselves. Indeed, they will have to do this in a family feud scenario. If the child has lived with the grandparents for at least three years (this period need not be continuous but must not have begun more than five years before, or ended three months before the making of the application) they are entitled either to join in or to start proceedings. They are similarly entitled if they have the consent of each of the persons having parental responsibility. If they are not entitled, they must seek the court's permission, which requires making a separate application to the court either to join in or to initiate proceedings.

- **Becoming the grandchild's special guardian (see before):** As in the case of residence orders, if the child has lived with the grandparents for at least three years (again, this period need not be continuous) they are entitled to apply to a court for a special guardianship order. This is a relatively new concept and was introduced in the Adoption and Children Act 2002. The idea is to provide carers and guardians with a more permanent legal responsibility over children who cannot live with birth parents but is one step short of adoption. The special guardianship order gives the guardian parental responsibility and is expected to last until the child is 18. It differs from an adoption order as parental responsibility still lies with the birth parents. It can allow a child, for example, previously in care to become the responsibility of the special guardian as opposed to the local authority. A special guardian has parental responsibility and is entitled to exercise that parental responsibility to the exclusion of any other person with parental responsibility. So although birth parents keep parental responsibility, the kind of major life decisions discussed in chapter 1 are made by the special guardian. Grandparents are similarly entitled to become special guardians if they have a residence order in their favour or if they have consent of each of the persons having parental responsibility for the child. If they are not entitled, they must seek the court's permission to make the application. Another requirement when applying for a special guardianship order is to give the local authority three months' written notice of the intention to make the application.

It is not always necessary to make an application since the court itself has the power to make a special guardianship order even where no application has been made. It could do this, for example, in section 8 proceedings or in care proceedings; but before doing so the judge must obtain a report from the local authority. In other words, in no circumstances can a special guardianship order be made without a local authority investigation and report. In deciding whether or not to make a special guardianship order the court must regard the child's welfare as the paramount consideration.

- **Adopting the grandchild:** One important change to the law (introduced by the Adoption and Children Act 2002) is that before grandparents can apply to adopt grandchildren they, like other relatives, must have provided a 'home' for the child for at least three years (under the previous law such a home only had to be provided for 13 weeks). This was a deliberate change to discourage grandparents (and other relatives) from seeking adoption orders and to encourage the use of other options such as special guardianship instead. Where grandparents have provided a 'home' for the child for the requisite period they, like other relatives, can apply to adopt. Like other relatives, grandparents are not subject to the requirement that the child must be placed by an adoption agency, so that an informal placement with them by the mother is perfectly lawful.

The courts do not readily make adoption orders in favour of grandparents, in part because if there is to be continued contact with the rest of the birth family, adoption seems inappropriate and in part because it distorts the legal relationships in that the grandparents become the parents and the parents become the siblings of the child. This predisposition not to make adoption orders in favour of grandparents is likely to have become greater with the availability of special guardianship and enhanced residence orders.

- **Applying to become a grandchild's guardian:** Another option open to grandparents is to apply to the court to become the child's guardian. This option will only be available if the child has no parent with parental responsibility for him or a residence order has been made with respect to the child in favour of a parent or guardian of his who has died while the order was in force.

In other words, applications can only be made where both married parents or an unmarried mother (and the unmarried father, too, if he has parental responsibility) are dead or on the death of a parent in whose favour a residence order has been made. In these circumstances, grandparents would be better advised to seek to become a guardian rather than to obtain a residence order, because as a guardian they can withhold agreement to the child's adoption. They do not need to go to court at all if they have been appointed a guardian by the parent in his or her will, or in a signed and dated document. Such an appointment will normally take effect upon the death of parents with parental responsibility, but if an appointing parent had a residence order in their favour it takes effect upon the appointer's death.

Who financially supports your children on a break-up?

On the breakdown of a relationship, you are both responsible for financially supporting the children irrespective of where they are living. (If you are married, you can also apply for spousal maintenance or financial support, whether you have children or not. If you aren't married, then your ex doesn't have to pay you maintenance for your own benefit, even if you've given up work to look after the children or your home, but will still have to pay child support.)

You can apply for maintenance through the courts, the Child Maintenance and Enforcement Commission (formerly the Child Support Agency) or you can agree your own arrangements. This is the body responsible for assessing and collecting payments for children who are under 16 years (or in full-time secondary education).

When a marriage ends you can apply for what is known as 'ancillary relief', which can take the form of regular payments (maintenance), one-off payments (lump sums), transfers of property or a share of your spouse's pension. Some divorcing couples can sort out their own financial issues between themselves. However, they might need some help to know what arrangement is fair. There are no clear rules so different views are likely to be taken as to what is appropriate. Further complications exist because the court will expect to see the agreement written up in technical language in a particular way. If nothing is done to formalise the agreement, then the claims might be left open to be pursued at a later date. It is a good idea to instruct solicitors for help so that any agreement is drawn up properly.

The legal processes of divorce and sorting the finances are not resolved at the same time or speed. When people complain about divorces dragging on for years, they generally mean that finances take a long time to sort rather than the relatively short length of time to obtain the divorce. So it could be that there is a decree absolute and your finances have yet to be finalised. A spouse's right to apply to the court regarding finances is lost on remarriage and so you must be careful to apply for ancillary relief before remarrying.

The legal principles that govern finances on divorce are covered in the Matrimonial Causes Act 1973, section 25 – see below. There is no straightforward formula for financial settlements post-divorce. Professional advice should be taken.

There has been much in the media about 'big money' divorces and, in particular, the theme of divorcees increasingly winning a half-share of their former partner's income. A few years ago the House of Lords shook up divorce law in the 2000 case of *White v White* when it established that the contributions of a 'homemaker' were equally valid to the building up of assets by the breadwinner. The Whites were a wealthy farming couple who built up a £4.6 million business over 33 years. After the split, Mrs White claimed an equal share of the business so she could continue to work. The Law Lords ruled that payouts had to reflect the circumstances of each case, but suggested that courts arrive at their assessment and then compare this against 'a yardstick of equality'. Since that ruling, the papers have followed 'big money' divorces, often featuring mothers who sacrificed careers for family; for example, the former City lawyer who was married for 16 years to a senior partner at an accountancy firm earning over £750,000 a year. The couple agreed she should give up her own high-flying career to raise their three children. The Laws Lords agreed that she was entitled to £250,000 a year for life as well as having child maintenance of £60,000. The reality is that these rulings concern a minority of the very wealthy. Most couples who break up are of more limited means; this often means there isn't enough money for the housing and living needs of both exes and such a division is not possible.

The principle of financial provision on divorce is equality of division of all resources. However, fairness may require that there are good reasons to depart from that principle – especially if the accommodation needs of the parent with primary care of the children require more than 50 per cent.

Otherwise if needs are met by sharing, resources are divided into two categories. Those assets acquired during the marriage (income through employment and growth in property values) will often be divided equally. However, for other assets – for example, those acquired pre-marriage, inheritances, gifts and some post-separation assets – it will be easier to depart from the principle of equal division if good reason can be demonstrated. How much one departs from equality depends on many factors.

Matrimonial Causes Act 1973, section 25

It shall be the duty of the court in deciding whether to exercise its powers ... to have regard to all the circumstances of the case, first consideration being given to the welfare while a minor of any child of the family who has not attained the age of eighteen. As regards the exercise of the powers of the court ..., the court shall in particular have regard to the following matters:

a) the income, earning capacity, property and other financial resources which each of the parties to the marriage has or is likely to have in the foreseeable future;

b) the financial needs, obligations and responsibilities which each of the parties to the marriage has or is likely to have in the foreseeable future;

c) the standard of living enjoyed by the family before the breakdown of the marriage;

d) the age of each party to the marriage and the duration of the marriage;

e) any physical or mental disability of either of the parties to the marriage;

f) the contributions which each of the parties has made or is likely in the foreseeable future to make to the welfare of the family, including any contribution by looking after the home or caring for the family;

g) the conduct of each of the parties;

h) the value to each of the parties to the marriage of any benefit (e.g. a pension) which, by reason of the dissolution or annulment of the marriage, that party will lose the chance of acquiring.

How did the Child Support Agency operate?

Each parent is responsible for maintaining their child (under the Child Support Act 1991). The issue of child support is incredibly complicated and a politically fraught issue which is (at the time of going to press) in the process of being overhauled.

The Matrimonial Causes Act 1857 first gave courts the power not only to grant divorce but also to award financial support to provide for the maintenance and education of children. The 1991 Act meant that for the first time maintenance had to be calculated by reference to a formula which took into account the financial circumstances of each parent. Parents with whom the children normally lives ('parents with care') who were on welfare benefits were effectively forced to make an application to the CSA for maintenance or have their benefits cut.

The Child Maintenance and Enforcement Commission, which in 2008 took over responsibility for the CSA, has authority to act where:

- you or your ex live separately from your child;

- you are a 'parent' (natural, adopted or conceived as a result of IVF);

- your child is under 16 years or in full-time secondary education; and

- your child is living in the UK or the absent parent ('non-resident parent') lives in the UK.

The old formula

The original Child Support Act set out the 'old formula', which took into account the non-resident parent's income and housing costs and the parent with care's income, housing costs and other children. The old formula is still in force for pre-2003 claims. The CSA also took into account the number of overnight stays the children had with the non-resident parent and their new children, pension contributions and new partner's earnings. The parent with care's natural children, pension contribution and new partner earnings were also taken into account.

It was always recognised that the inflexibility of a formula could deliver unfair results and so you could make an application giving the CSA the right to 'depart' from it. Such an application could take into consideration, for example, costs of travelling to work, contact costs (e.g. the expense of the costs of travel to see a child), costs relating to illness or disability, debts incurred before the parents separated, as well as transfers of capital made on divorce. There were other protections and so if a non-resident parent deliberately paid income to another party to evade the CSA that would be taken into account, or if their lifestyle was inconsistent with declared income.

The process of calculating maintenance has proved complex, and according to CSA critics, cumbersome and time-consuming. It was reckoned over 100 separate pieces of information were needed before an assessment could be calculated.

Uncollected arrears of maintenance began to arise and by 2006 those arrears amounted to over £3.5 billion. In a landmark legal challenge a mother, called Mary Kehoe, claimed that, as a result of the agency's errors, maintenance was lost. She wanted the government to pay that loss. Her case went all the way to the House of Lords and it was ruled in 2005 that the parent with care had no right to take steps themselves to recover arrears of maintenance – and if the secretary of state did not use the discretionary powers available to recover maintenance arrears then a parent with care could not claim compensation.

Post-2003 formula

For many years Parliament attempted to improve the child support scheme. In particular, the Child Support Pensions and Social Security Act 2000 simplified the calculation process and introduced a new formula coming into effect as of March 2003.

The new formula operates along the following lines:

- establish income of the non-resident parent, deducting tax, National Insurance and pension contributions;

- deduct a set percentage for any new children living in the same household (15 per cent for one child, 20 per cent for two, and 25 per cent for three or more);

- determine a set percentage of the remaining income that has to be paid to the parent with care – 15 per cent for one child, 20 per cent for two, and 25 per cent for three or more; and

- then divide the resulting figure to reflect any overnight stays and so if a child stays with the non-resident parent one night a week then the maintenance would be reduced by one-seventh.

Under new legislation there will be changes to the formula, likely to happen in 2011 at the earliest. Critics of the CSA were not placated, though, and argue that even this new simplified formula has proved too difficult to implement and there have been calls for it to be abolished. One of the new roles of the Child Maintenance and Enforcement Commission is to encourage parents to make their own private arrangements with regard to maintenance to be paid, coupled with tougher enforcement powers if the non-resident parent fails to pay.

Details as to how to apply to the Child Maintenance and Enforcement Commission are included on its website. The CSA had a poor track record on collecting maintenance, but the new agency collected £1,132 million in the year ending June 2009, a record-breaking amount and a 42 per cent increase compared to 2005. If a non-resident parent doesn't pay, then the agency can take money direct from their earnings, bank accounts or take action through the courts. If there is a private agreement and the non-resident parent doesn't pay, you can contact the agency.

What happens to your home on a split?

The situation depends on whether or not you are married:

- **Unmarried couples:** If you are anxious about what will happen about your home on the break-up of your relationship, there are number of issues you need to consider:

  If your home is jointly owned, there could be a deed of trust (a written agreement) setting out your individual financial contributions and the shares in which you hold the property. If there is, the likelihood is that you will be bound by the terms of that agreement.

  If your home is jointly owned and there is no written agreement, as is often the case, you would normally hold as joint tenants (see before).

If your home is held in the sole name of your ex, then you could still be able to make a claim for a share of the property if you have made contributions to the purchase of the property, paid off the mortgage or helped pay it off, or paid for a new roof and a loft conversion. What is important is the intention of you and your ex and so if, for example, you intended to marry this would give a stronger inference that you intended to share the benefit of the property. For this reason, it is sensible if you aren't a co-owner to make direct payments towards the mortgage to establish an interest. If you are the parent with care, there are further options. As explained earlier in this chapter, you may be able to make an application under the Children Act 1989 for your ex to provide a new home, or make a contribution, where the children can live with you until they finish full-time education. You might also be able to prevent the sale of your home. There are various ways of doing this: your ex could own the property and be ordered to pay the mortgage, you could jointly own the property or the property could be in your name (as the parent with care) and your ex could have a second charge on the property to take into account a proportionate increase in value until the property is sold. Clearly one of the main factors here will be the financial circumstances of your ex.

- **Married couples:** The property where you live, even if it is in the sole name of your ex, becomes the 'matrimonial home' and you have rights to that property, including not to be evicted from the property without a court order. Assuming you do not own the property, you can place a married person's notice on the property preventing it from being sold without your knowledge in order to protect your rights. You should register that right at the Land Registry.

The matrimonial home is often the main financial asset – and the court's starting point, certainly, in a long marriage, is that assets should be shared equally.

You are living in rented accommodation and you are about to split – what happens?

- **Unmarried couples:** Whether you are joint tenants or the tenancy is in your ex's name only an application can be made (under the Family Law Act 1996) to court for a transfer of the tenancy into the other's. Notice has to be provided to the landlord in advance of the hearing, and there may be several hearings before a decision is reached. Most local authorities and housing associations do not recognise agreements to transfer the property from one person's name to another or from their joint names to a single name unless by a court order.

There are a number of factors which the court takes into account when dealing with an application to transfer a tenancy: its first concern will be if you have any children, and then if you are disabled, the basis upon which the tenancy was originally granted, whether there is alternative accommodation, as well as the chances of being re-housed by the local authority.

It is important that neither you nor your ex make yourselves 'intentionally homeless' by voluntarily leaving the property. To do so means that you are unlikely to be re-housed by the local authority even if you are in priority need. You should therefore only leave the property if forced to do so by a court order.

There are some tenancies left granted under the Rent Acts with private landlords. These tenants have considerable security and pay a protected 'fair rent', often considerably less than the market rent. You, or your ex, can hold the property on the same terms as the original tenant. The local authority would regard violence by your ex as an action making you intentionally homeless.

Is it possible to break up without falling out?

Yes. Divorcing couples often feel that they are pushed into opposing camps but there are approaches that help to achieve a conciliatory approach and a healthy working relationship after marriage.

Mediation can be useful for helping couples who are splitting but who want to sort out their own affairs albeit with some help. It isn't like marriage counselling, an attempt to get back you together. But it is an opportunity to sit down with someone properly trained to help. A mediator will meet with you and your ex, together or separately, to identify the issues; work out where each party stands; and fill out forms and, if possible, put together a document covering the areas of agreement. It is crucial (and part of their training) that a qualified mediator should not make decisions for you and they should not take sides. If you are on legal aid, then you have to consider mediation before you can get public funding. You don't have to go through mediation; you only have to consider it. If you are not on legal aid, a mediator can be a lot cheaper than a solicitor and can cut down on the final legal costs considerably.

At the end of the mediation process a summary document is drawn up which sets out the points that you and your ex have agreed. It is not in itself legally binding. However, as far as it relates to finances after divorce, or arrangements for children, you can ask the court to make your agreement legally binding. As described above, a solicitor will often be needed to help you with this. A document called a draft consent order will be sent to the court. A judge will look at it and decide whether to make the order.

'Collaborative law' is something else you might hear about. It is totally separate from mediation. The expression describes a relatively new approach by family lawyers to manage the divorce process in a potentially less stressful and sometimes more cost-effective manner. In a collaborative approach you work with your lawyers to agree in writing to reach settlement without court involvement. You have to agree to work together to resolve children's and financial issues arising from the separation. You have to have the kind of relationship with your ex where you can bear to sit around the table with them and their lawyer. You and your ex agree with your lawyers to resolve issues without going to court through a series of face-to-face meetings (you, your lawyer, your ex plus their lawyer). If no settlement can be reached or either party makes a court application, each has to instruct new lawyers for court proceedings.

What if you have been assaulted and threatened by your partner – can you take legal action to protect yourself and your children?

Yes. There are a range of orders the courts can make to try to prevent further problems such as injunctions to keep your partner away from you or out of your house. Sometimes such orders can be obtained very quickly and without your partner (it is usually the man but not always) finding out that you are going to court. You should see a solicitor specialising in family law (preferably one registered with the Law Society's Family Law Accreditation Scheme).

Can you stop a violent partner from living at your jointly rented home?

Yes; but a 'notice to quit' given by one joint tenant brings the whole tenancy to an end. Some landlords will agree to let a victim of domestic violence do this and then enter a new tenancy in your sole name immediately thereafter. Speak to your landlord first. But don't give notice to quit if you are unsure of what the consequences will be for you.

You need to move out of your home to get away from your violent partner. What help can you get from the council to get re-housed?

If you have children and have left your home to escape violence from your partner, it is likely that your local council will have a responsibility to accommodate you. You will need to contact its homelessness department and tell it that you need to make an application to it as a homeless person. In most such cases your council will have a duty to give you accommodation straight away if needed even before it has reached a final decision on what exactly to do with you.

The council will have to bear in mind your need to get away from your partner when it decides where to re-house you. The law relating to homelessness and re-housing can be complex. If you have difficulties in dealing with your council – for example, if it refuses to accept your application or if you can't understand the decision it has reached on your case – then you should see a solicitor specialising in housing law as soon as possible.

How do the police handle an allegation of domestic violence?

The priority for police officers dealing with an allegation of domestic violence is to ensure the safety of all persons at the scene. They should speak to the victim and take an account of the incident, keeping her separate from the suspect to enable her to speak freely. Victims should also be informed about the support services available to them. Police officers are responsible for taking statements from the victim and any other witnesses. Children (and in some cases adults) will be interviewed on video by trained officers and this video will usually become their evidence in chief in any subsequent trial.

Cases are referred at an early stage to the Crown Prosecution Service (CPS). It will then decide whether to charge the suspect with any criminal offence. Incidents of domestic violence often give rise to charges of assault but there may be other charges (e.g. harassment).

If the defendant denies the offence, the case will then be listed for a trial before magistrates or in more serious cases before a judge and jury. It can take some time for trials to come around and in many cases defendants will be granted bail while they await trial. It is CPS practice to request that conditions (e.g. non-contact with witnesses) are attached to bail in order to protect victims and witnesses.

The CPS decides whether to prosecute and may proceed with a prosecution even where the victim withdraws her support. In appropriate cases the CPS may apply to the court for a witness summons or even an arrest warrant to ensure that a reluctant or frightened witness attends court. More commonly the court will grant 'special measures' (e.g. you can speak via videolink or there will be screens to avoid eye contact) to assist a witness in giving evidence. All magistrates' and Crown Courts have a witness support service, which offers help to witnesses.

Defendants convicted of an offence involving domestic violence may be sentenced to a range of penalties, from a fine to imprisonment. Judges also have the power in appropriate cases to make compensation orders, restraining orders and anti-social behaviour orders.

CONTACTS

Living together

For more information on where you can marry and what you have to do to get married, see the General Register Office (www.gro.gov.uk) and the Church of England (www.cofe.anglican.org) sites. For advice on cohabitation, see the Advice Now guide (www.advicenow.org.uk/living-together). For more information about civil partnerships, see gay and lesbian rights group Stonewall (www.stonewall.org.uk).

For information about family law and to find a family law solicitor, see the family lawyers' group Resolution (www.resolution.org.uk). To find out more about the intestacy rules, see the Citizens Advice Bureau's site (www.adviceguide.org.uk).

Living apart

For advice and support on relationship breakdown, see the marriage counselling service Relate (www.relate.org.uk).

There is useful information on the legal process of divorce on the Court Service's website (www.hmcourts-service.gov.uk), where you can download all the relevant forms and see also the CAFCASS site (www.cafcass.gov.uk).

For help on grandparents and contact, see www.grandparents-association.org.uk.

To find out more about mediation, see the Family Mediation Helpline (www.familymediationhelpline.co.uk).

For more information on collaborative law, see the Resolution site (www.resolution.org.uk).

To find a lawyer specialising in domestic violence cases, see www.communitylegaladvice.org.uk. For information on the conduct of the police in domestic violence cases, see the Association of Chief Police Officers Guidance on Investigating Domestic Abuse 2008 and www.acpo.police.uk/policies.asp.

Index